I've been to Venus & back
These Are Real Feelings
Let the Universe Guide Your Heart
through Space

Sunny Jetsun

'The human brain is made up of 100 billion neurons and nearly 100 trillion synapses. There are 300 times more connections in the brain than there are stars in the Milky way galaxy.' Resonance Project.

*

Cover Image by: Laurie Caradonna
Image has been color shifted and resized
Used and Distributed as ShareAlike Under Creative Commons License:
https://creativecommons.org/licenses/by-sa/2.0/

Mandala & Final Page Art by: Sophie Starseed

Dedicated to those living in the 'ASD * BPD' spectrum of Cosmic space
And to the whistleblowers sharing the Truth * Love*Light

*I've been to Venus & back*These Are Real Feelings*
*Let the Universe Guide Your Heart*through Space*

Other Books by Sunny Jetsun:
'driving my scooter through the asteroid field
Coming down over Venus ~ "Hallo Baba"'
'Light love Angels from Heaven. New Generation, Inspiration,
Revolution, Revelation ~ All the colours of Cosmic Rainbows'
'Green Eve * Don't lose the Light Vortex *
My brain's gone on holiday ~ free flowing feelings'
'Surfing or Suffering ~ together * Sense Consciousness
fields of a body with streams and stars of hearts'
"When You're happy you got wings on your back ~
Reposez vos oreilles a Goa; We're only one kiss away"
'PSYCHIC PSYCHEDELIC'
'Streaming Lemon Topaz Sunbeams'
'Invasion of Beauty * FLASH * The Love Mudras'
'Patchouli Showers ~ Tantric Temples'
'It's Just a Story, We Are All the Sun, Sweet Surrender'
Anthology #1 ~ 'Enjoy The Revolution'
Anthology # 2 ~ 'Love & Freedom ~ Welcome'
'He Lives In A Parallel Universe'
'Queen of Space, King of Flower Power ~ dripping rainbows'
'All Love Frequency ~ In Zero Space'
*Peace Goddess*Spirit of the Field*The Intimacy Sutras*
*Heavenly Bodies ~ Celestial Alignments
Feeling ~ Energy that Is LOVE in Itself*

Sunny Jetsun Online at:
Website: www.sunnyjetsun.com
Facebook: www.facebook.com/sunnyjetsun
Smashwords:www.smashwords.com/profile/view/sunnyjetsun
Amazon: www.amazon.com/author/sunnyjetsun

*Empathic * Smile*

That's gorgeous, beautiful by its simplicity and deep truth
Respecting the right of other people to worship their 'sacred' source ~
With the knowing that they would do the same for you as it's All Spiritual!
Understanding that we are all a point sharing and transmuting in the same
*holistically *****Conscious *****Cosmic Space frequency*

*

5th Dimensional Energy Is Reflecting Sacred Earth

Indigenous INDIGOS V Corporate Mafias' Sociopathic Bully Boys!
Fighting back against Genocidal, Imperial Governments; 'Colonise,
destroy, move on progression!' Ground Zero on the War on Nature;
Deforestation, War on Water, Toxic Streets run along Pesticide Lake ~
Air & water on which all life depends becoming a Global rubbish dump!
*No man is an Island * Giving back the lust of her beloved full love Moon.*
*'Global citizens we are Protectors not Protesters'*Unity Consciousness.*
Need detachment of Mind to delete the illusory ~ the Cosmic betrayer.
When you're sleeping your dreams are real ~ Wake up now!
Rhythm ~ coming, going together, sharing energy, changing.
The artist and the super muse ~ Putting the strokes into her.

*

The Locked-In Syndrome

Smiling is dangerous ~ sometimes; Yeah you're right!
"Can't even predict what you're going to do!"
"It's a Power trip not a Spiritual trip.
"It's a Commercial World" He said.
You can dance your music because
You're vibrating in your cells.

*

"It's a Big Sky!"
The Golden Ray
*In a field of iridescent blue * turquoise peacocks.*
'Wild Game'

<u>Deep Attachments</u>
'No empathy ~ No feeling or remorse.'
They sacrifice their own people!
Machines - they lost their blood.
* Jumping between dimensions *
Let go and another light comes
*

<u>Your Brain Is Constructing Reality</u>
You are Your Self ~ the best refraction*reflection in town.
"You are a bio*genome product of God knows what!"
He lost heart. The Universe forgives you; Be Painless.
Too busy to be depressed! Life is a continuous Party!
We all have the chance to make the World a nicer place!
Creativity is that which is all around ~ Life is Spiritual.
Tibet was once the strongest of the strong in Dhamma.
Jesus was an Open Source Activist ~ arriving in the free
Cosmic * Spatial.
*

<u>"You were a Mango Baby!"</u>
"You're in Love with the World"
Product of a Love marriage ~
brought up free to be what I wanted to be.
Mind fed with emotion ~ Siddhartha renounced his family!
Polyhymnia the muse of sacred poetry relaxing
in the nude by an infinity pool. ~ Love like Heroin,
the biggest hook can catch the deepest feelings!'
We've all been there, written books of hymns and Zen rhymes,
Sufi Haiku, Intimacy Sutras, Painful sonnets, Magical mantras.
Is there one to make a woman fall in love with you forever?
Do you want that? Of course I want that! So you have that &
I'll have that then OK? "I'll be your slave to the end of time!"
Circumstances change nothing lasts in the multidimensional.

Grow * Bulbs
Genetically designed to go through a DMT. wormhole!
*Common-sense ~ Devotion to the Planet * Mother Earth.*
Your Mother dying, the biggest existential loss in your life!
What parents need to know about Monsanto.
'By 2025 one in two children will be Autistic.'
The War Against the Insurgents, "leave and we'll shoot you!"
'If you see hell comin' you get out of the way'
Ultimately it's to become Conscious

*

Go * Goa * Gaia * Tree
'Smoking pot is slavery to vegetables; God will set you free!'
Said we're partying to the end ~ beyond sunrise, past sunset.
Yogi Love ~ detached Sannyasin, doing some meditation.
"You don't wanna depend on her for your Happiness!"
"She can't give you that ~ it's Your Mind's Expectations & desires"
*Maya's fantastical distractions * fabulous dreams, fears & delusion.*
"Someone you know who Loves you is here in front of your eyes ~
and you don't feel it, recognise it, are even conscious of it, want it!"
You've switched it off, let it drown, you have thrown away this Jewel.
You've rejected a rare bliss! Do you know what you're doing; Why?

*

Cricket Widows
Start Observing the Mind ~ MA giving birth.
Sunny skies on the way along a razor's horizon.
Direct this energy into feelings of the Heart's art.
Yogi paradox ~ "Smile at every Goddess that smiles at you"
Conscious of having the deepest, strongest, unbound feelings.
It's Not the Fuck it's about LOVE ~ Soul to Soul attraction.
"Women are able to deal with more pain than men!"
Physical & emotional ~ Becoming EGOLESS
'The Universe Loves Me'

3

It's Your Karma Cleaner
Why is it so Important Being In Love?
Life feels like beautiful poetry ~ You hurt me!
On the laser's edge of time not under her Ego.
"You need a foreign car to get a date with them!"
Letting thoughts go ~ taking charge of your Mind
changing its course ~ don't wanna be mowed down!
Can't feel the love in my eyes, heart, in her multi orgasms!
Love is immaterial ~ What Ego have you got to fuck with!
'May All beings Love one another'

*

Point Blank
She's a Sniper ~ Shot me in the head!
'Energy that can't ever be destroyed * dead'
Let go of the Image ~ "You mean nothing"
All about TRUSTING * enlightening the Pain.
They're dramatic, extreme, reacting to all of it!
Cravings of feeling fear ~ Love is inside you.
Nothing but projections rattling in our brain.
Love Is Always there ~

*

Full Nature Reflection
Feeling Itself through us ~
'Life Force is experiencing Life
as a Sentient Human Being ~ Intuition'
Immersed, absorbed in the Garden of Eden.
It's all there in front of me and I can't see it!
Love It Always ~ Open hearted free spirit Space.
That's Life ~ Feeling its Sensations equanimously.

AC. Shopping Malls

It's much too hot in the desert ~ blinded by EGO!
We love the UFO on the Highway ~ lets You decide.
Try and develop the Awareness ~ keeping it fresh.
The Universe Loves me even if I'm a nobody to you.
"I love you but I need you to make me happy Baby!"
You can't give that Ultimate Power to someone else!
She loves me I'm her Darling ~ becoming Love overflow.
You start loving her ~ turning into Cosmic, Open Love.
"She's just a branch of the tree" ~ being Detached.
Someone you Love to Love and she's reflecting it ~
Where is this person who loves you? "I don't know"
"She's cheating ~ Love should be selfless; No shoulds!
"I LOVE YOU" ~ Full Stop! Fearless, Absolute, Freely

*

INVIOLATE TRUST

Babe in arms letting the mother decide ~
gives you the wheel of the car ~ blanked out.
Don't want to think about it ~ it's too painful.
You're the Observer, it's just another fairy tale.
You're only a character performing on the stage.
The story becomes real while you're reading it!
You go back into that Space ~ Your Space, changed me.
I found his Omnipresent Love Inside my suffering ~
Whether the face changes is destiny but Love won't go.
I like being in Love ~ flowers blossoming in a summer meadow,
Nymphaea lily ponds and gardeners watering the Rose garden.
Disintegration of this Love Program, it's over, out yur depth!
A big realisation, you become a better Lover in detachment.
Experiences ~ I am reflecting everything for the best I can.
"A good human being doesn't play with other's emotions."
"She's lying, you wouldn't want her as Queen of your life."

People Taking It All too Sirius!

"Because It Matters to the Mind
It only knows Things ~ Not Space!"
Limited to the Identification of things.
You Are the Eternal Presence in Life
That's what Life Is.
If You Conceptualise Life ~ you lose its Essence.
Overriding the Mind, recognizing other people as
Themselves ~ same same different * Life force.
Feeling empathy ~ 'In La kech'
All the World's problems ~ Seeing
the Madness thing in My own Mind!
'This is a FoRm of Life appearing to me'
*

Her Pure Heart ~ she married St Valentine.
Living a gigantic Fantasy through the head.
A beautiful idea of a Prince Most Charming.
Not a Genghis Khan, Sun King or Black Pope!
*** A Collection of Emotions ***
Her field of dreams living inside me.
'Going through Life ~
The Point Is to Observe!'
Can become a Possessive entity ~ ME.
Accumulation of "This is f..... Mine!"
In the Brain's * Association* there's Magical existence.
Altered experience with certain Conditioned Things.
War & Torture! Surviving the Dissociation Syndrome.
'Fulfillment not what you do but how you do it'
Can I be Aware of Actually being Aware?'
In honoring the Present moment.

In Our *Biophoton *Consciousness
All Thought is FORM we have in this World.
'Beyond this Mental-FORM IS the FORMLESS'
The SPACE ~ Inside Us * holistic Awareness.
You are the Generator of the thought not the 'Object' of it.
Just seeing the thoughts in the head nothing to do with ME.
Not believing ME is in the thoughts, telling ME I'm Un/happy!
Identifying with this Play not realising it's a Program in Ego's Theatre.
Are you Conscious of Yourself dreaming in reality ~ time passing.
Still left in the moment, transforming ~ all part of that Big de/illusion.
Just sitting in the Silence ~ Spaces feeling Inner Universal Stillness.

*

Tantric Polyhymnia
The muse of sacred poetry with the languid daughters of Zeus.
Your energy's crash diving can't pull out of the G force spirals!
Connect light in electronic signals, mesmerized, broke all trust.
Another egotistic, haughty, disdainful, aloof, resentful ladybird.
Needs more energetic healing ~ which gives life its meaning.
Soothing love pulling you out of a black hole electro*magnetically.
Free surrendering your will to my divine Angel of Love ~ vibes.
Give it to someone who understands you, adores you selflessly.
Someone who simply cares, right? She don't give a fuck, Why?
Betrayal, cheating yourself ~ She cheated you out of happiness.
SPACED OUT.

*

Sri Yantra Mandala
It's back to front, cooked the books; Pull the trigger, spray!
'Nice' why not make it More Nice! No Heavy swords & Amour.
Coerced treasure, diamonds from them * Apsaras all around!
Spiritual power not just muscle power ~ Perceiving Mind.
Surrendering to the Cock-a-doodle-do in my sound field.
Conceptions making Space into an Object ~ USHINISHA.

7

<u>Being In Love</u>
You can't try you just are ~
The Realisation that 'You Are'.
That it is the Still *Silent *Space
Inside us is Universal
Reflection of all things, the tides ~ of I Om
with one nothingness * Is pure Consciousness.
Shine through Baba it's a beautiful feeling of joy.
Magicness because of this clear Awareness ~ finally!
'Life coming in ~ Death going out into the Cosmic Ocean'
Transformation of the Spirit into a light * shining through.
'Focus Attention on energy*real currency feeding our Planet'
The FORM dis/appears but the SPACE is Always there ~
We think we're Individual but we're ALL FREE SPIRIT
"I'd like to see a Miracle." "You are the Miracle if you,
truly see all things as a Miracle ~ they are Miraculous."
Such a deep mystery to surrender to when you see the light.
* Angels in a Wonderland World ~ all over *
Why wouldn't you witness such a beauty?
If you like it you have it, Love it.
Surrendering to Cosmic Orgasms!
In the moment ~ Can't Control It
*

<u>Illusionist * Telepathy</u>
How to see past the Inhuman Pain and Suffering.
Beginning to believe in Spirit*Soul not in Oblivion.
Left the factory making drones and sentient clones.
A Tyrannical System benefitting Lucifer's Despots!
Is it in your blood to be Free or Not to be <> Enslaved?
Look into my eyes, consequences of your Objective intent.
Trusting my gut feelings, intuition ~ your soul, it was right!
'Protect Happiness' look after the seeds and baby giraffes!

8

Golden Soma

Wisdom and empowerment are the gifts of Satya's Yuga.
Cherry Goddess of Transformation*Self's destruct button!
Maya is desire, Matrix duality*Desireless is Cosmic Space.
"I hope you get what you're looking for Baby Karma of Kali"
Just desserts in an unjust system, what do you know of Soul?
What's your concept of Freedom and Slavery Master?
'Il est defendu de marcher sur la pelouse.' So Fuck off!
Conditioned for a set of limits ~ limits that are our delusions.
Realise All is forbidden! No boundaries to be transcended?
"I know there is no Separation and it's all a Super illusion!"
My existence is beyond a body-mind sense-field hologram.
Space is Formless ~The Mind cannot compute 'Nothingness'
It can only buy a pig for a bloody guinea and send it to Mars!

*

Transcending Kleptocracy

"You need desire to be a better person"
I don't wanna feel oppressed; Try 250 mikes never the same again!
In my mind, wash of the bottle was fantastic, everything is very surreal,
beautiful, colours jumping out of people's heads; A Kundalini power ray!
Stalked by a woman in Cambodia, escaped from the Sevak in Persia!
'Laos had more Bombs dropped on it than any other country in history!'
Was done clandestinely, homicidal, ask Henry Kissinger's chiefs of staff.
More Genocidal Bombing than on Germany And Japan in World War 2!
Ask a bipolar pensioner studying Psychology what he thinks of
Political power using electric shock to torture! & Ask any Despot!
Every instant is essentially changing as electricity in a light ~
The illusion to my limited eye*sight is that it is constantly there!
Everything lives in cycles ~ dematerialises into Cosmic Oceans.
"Why did you travel to the end of the World?" "I came for Love."

9

Persian Delight ~ Spinning Space

Your Ego goes your Consciousness lives on from Mind/body ~
Reflections of photons shining on your DNA*lights up a crystal.
Artificially created Self-Mind*Enjoying Unconscious Moments.
A Mental-Form Identity, ME then it's a Separated framework
of a Isolated Individual*State. Strapped 'ME' into the head!
If you can fly out of hallucinations * Psychedelic Spaceman.
'You Are Conscious Space' material Is happening in a brain
making Mind-Forms, Conditioning; 'That's MY toy, fuck off!'
Birth of the Ego ~ I own it; How when it all comes & goes?
OK it's Cosmic to let it go in Peace & Love not hate & War.
All stems from thoughts in your head so we're led to believe.
Realising duality < running from Fear > running to Desire!
Happening in those genetic procreation boxes so on & on.
Amplified patterns of emotions*thoughts in your body-mind.
Thoughts generating my Love for You seem so real now.
It's an Illusion otherwise we wouldn't have smashed apart.
Really Love Is Love ~ essence of who we are & together.
POINT of INFINITY * LOVING LOVE * UNIVERSALITY
*

Psychedelic Chandeliers

Baptising a goose in the Garden of Earthly Delights.
What does it mean? Whatever you want it to mean.
"I don't want anything hard in my heart!"
Why do without it if you can do with it?
His girlfriend ended up going off with a footballer.
What are the colours and feelings of a Sufi Mantra,
vibrations of LSD-25? ~ 'Whirl in, turn on, drop out'
"Woman needs to feel love to have sex
Men need to have sex to feel love"
Have a double drop in energy fields of Life.
250 mgms. Out of Mind * hard to let go & ~
Experience a really great trip.

Your Energetic Essence
Dr. Timothy Leary asked Sandoz for a litre of LSD 25.
'And they gave it to him?' 'No.' Can't get my head around it.
Punks didn't like hippies. He's not a hippy he's Psychedelic!
Went to see the Sex Pistols, Johnny Rotten spat in his face!

*

Prime Mate Seeds
Cosmic infinite is Formless ~ meaningless
All concepts in your Mind's perceiving, right from wrong duality?
God should definitely have forgiven his Tantric devotees by now!
Returning to live in Love in the Garden of Paradise if they feel it
Is the Happy choice.

*

Deflowering without a rusty Gillette
Opening the soft petals of a Peonie
The winning sperm * crowned 'Daddy'
Starting to develop the brain inside the embryo
Your heart starts beating on the 18th day before the brain
First heart rhythm of life ~~~~

*

The Blackest Hole Paradox
When you got nothing to lose ~
Then how can you lose nothing?
There's always Something, Mind*Creations.
"These dreams were a real f.... nightmare!"
Is outside a reflection of inside*vice versa?
We're an integral part of it all not Separate.
We're the same * Universal FORMS APP.
Making twinkling stars and Planets spin ~
Attachment to each Mind-moment not to a
holy, burning, glowing, crashing meteorite
falling to Earth ~ drowned in the Ocean!
"It takes you on a Cosmic trip my dream"
'You feeling your Love in your heart'

<u>Joining the cast from Hell, 100% Guilty, why be in any doubt?</u>
'James Holmes is believed to have killed 12 people attending a
midnight screening of a Batman movie; Mr Breivik is Alleged to…
Is it Psychological warfare, Subliminal messaging into your brain?
'Win a year's worth of Free electricity' from a Righteous Authority!
Who is writing this Propaganda and putting it on the front pages?
A billion hedge funds subdivided UK landscape, field/Separation.
Is there such a thing as a 'Popular War'? Call that Duty a Horror!
Who's ordering you to commit terrible Crimes Against Humanity?
Why do it? Comply or be an imprisoned Conscientious Objector ~
or one of Shot at Dawn brigade! Driving your Mind-soul to pasture.

*

<u>Good things come back ~</u>
"The Fundamental delusion of humanity is to suppose
that I am here and you are out there." Yasutani Roshi.
'Australia, until 1960s, Aborigines came under the Flora &
Fauna Act, classified them as animals, not human beings.'
'Who is stimulating Ego ~ left brain function, suppressing
'heart-mind,' intuition and creative Life inspiration,' Why?
The Notes of C *Heart chakra & A *Crown chakra, 432hz!
Music is the sound of your sensory feelings in flow ~ Why
desynchronize humans from their Universal frequency?
Spending your Precious life's ~ time doing what?
"It's a weed; Plant a seed wherever you can!"
"We didn't grow it ~ Mother Nature did!"
"I like Escapism not Realism." "STOP IT Now!"
Kali do you get scared if I touch you too much?
Calling a woman your Lovely Rainbow ~
If she's good she's naturally Orgasmic
Everyone's truly Cosmic.

Disenchanted Community

Poverty <.> Propertytrap@RevolutionaryTime ~ dynamics.com.
Problem of .1% of the haves and 99.99999% of the have nots!
Listening to 'The Mental Madness of Violence' on the car radio,
day after 'illegal shooting' of Dr, Martin Luther King in Alabama.
"Violence breeds violence, repression brings retaliation"
Ask the doomsday Politicos and Weapons' Warmongers!
A series of Assassinations, why not dream of Inspiration?
'The World could be a better place' ~ That day will come!
"She was in the ballroom when the shots rang out"
'Did it Open Up your Mind?' Looking into your heart & soul ~
Exquisite Sensitivity, the eloquence of feeling; a Passion Play
not bedlam or Mayhem ~ In shock, prone on the floor, dying!
"She's in tremendous pain but no awareness." Have Faith,
honour, not for that deranged, angry, brain washed murderer!
'Your enemy is my friend', fighting for your basic civil rights with
blazing guns, slaughtering all the dreamings of Peace Accords.
When will this 'Unpopular War' end? Ask the 'Unpopular dead!'
This person deserves to die, all illusion~hinging on emotional Ego!
Negativity, hate, anger, despair, destroys LOVE in the Mind*Heart.
'Own a piece of Paradise for less than you think'
Snakes following the vibration ~

*

Apsara * Heavenly Grace

Wow whatever happened to you? Possessed by a Dakshini!
'Be Aware of what you're wishing for' ~ Bottom of the Ocean.
In the end You showed me your black heart, who you were.
No light, no feelings, no consciousness, fully ignorant Ego!
Her Self-suicidal hormones * not Trusting, killing my Spirit.
Emotions wading through a deep depression in the desert.
No Star fields, no Oasis, no true heart to guide a traveler.
Shiva Valley all night trance ~ "We got the Chemicals!"

Illumined Quantum Monopoly
See the Plans * It's not unplugged!
It's a Control System, The Enemy.
The Truth veiled by a heavy curtain.
Your brain makes Dreams Real.
Sentient clones*Matrix Authority.
Trying to Free our Mind, World
And let all the Paranoiac Fears go ~
She looks lovely, another concept, Illusion.
Memories telling me my life history, 'I Am'.
Holograms fixing me * in timeless space.

*

Genome Fabricant
Drones & Clones belonging to Tyrannical Systems.
Hate in your heart, its venom only destroys you!
'To know thyself is only possible through
eyes' ~ clear reflections from another'
Consequences of Intent & reaction.
The beloved * that Love was Real!
Bound together forever & ever ~
Creating the present moment Amen.
Revolution * Realisation * Revelation.
Shining the Truth into ~ the brightest Light in Space.
Finding the Highest Love to Transcend all our Infatuation!

*

Spiked Banana Bread!
"We do have glorious Angels looking, watching over us"
Authoritarian Police State ~ In Fear, running for their lives!
'Order and Progress' ~ 'Nature and Chaos', Artistic, Activistic.
Blowing itself to bits, killing its own people! Where was that?
That's the Rule! 5000 Rupees you can get a hitman!

Believing She's Real

Letting it happen, letting her go not chasing an Apsara's chimera ~
A couple who wanna be in Love; 'If its got Form its got Limits Baby!
You believe a perspective in the Mind which is creating an Illusion....
Nexus 7, "A Capitalist wet-dream because you're asleep to believe it"
Switch-off brain's delusional thinking * EGO needs its Limits of Duality
for its own Existence*To keep us falling in delusion. Everything she said
was bullshit; You'll never understand what really makes things happen!
Mad but it happened, differently, forgive, be happy and let her f.... go!
Say 'I don't know' Open ~ Knowing is but the Mind * limiting paradigm.
When will the Manifestation of EGO rear up? D'yu know what I mean?
"Tongue right down my throat and I was sitting in an empty room!"
Eternity is the absence of time ~ not in realms of Compu-Turing.
A game of gain & loss of Existence ~ 'I'm right, you're wrong!'
Sunrise * Sunset we're all spinning around the Sun of the Sun*
The loss occurs in your Inner Space * Space that's always there ~
See it as Mind-projection*coming & going ~ Knowing Impermanence.
Experience it to know that Everything will lose You, it's ever changing!
Delusion thinks that the next moment is better than the moment NOW.
Underlying of Attachment * Transmuting the whole thing from Totality.
Projects Ourselves in Mind-games, past, memory * future, Imagination.
Apart from that it has No Existence ~ yet Stillness is always there!
Invisible Zero Space * is Infinite * No limits * Knowing the illusional.
"Helping restore the lost balance or letting things take their course?"
INFINITE IS FORMLESS * Mind can't get it that FORM Is temporary!
Get rid of smart 'Object' go to the boundless * Feelings of Life is Bliss.
UNCONDITIONAL * LOVE ~ Eternal * Essence not a craving Ego!
MIND can't grasp the Formless concept~ Feel Magic not the Fear!
Don't become Attached because You Are Already It * In Feelings.
Enjoying a harmonious moment * Happy Cosmic dancing frequency.

<u>Chelo Moscow</u>
"She thinks she can only take the fruit
without watering the roots!"
You've lost your feathers
Spaced out ~ in togetherness.
'You being in your creative moment'
"You're in this World and not of it"
Not being a human ~ one with life in time.
Be Conscious ~ everything becomes as it is.
The Bliss chemicals bouncing around the cortex.
Super natural high medicine not Fear ~ mongering!
We're all in the same boat somehow ~ Samadhi waves.
*

<u>Her Pink Full Moon Lit-Up!</u>
Sacrifice of a female collapsed brain * becoming whole again.
Helios' orbit connecting with the Central Cosmogyral SUN.
"We're going through this Galactic alignment"
"My daughter's got Seven planets in Scorpio"
900,000 years of DNA existing ~ "Don't put Your Self in it!"
Who lends the Illuminati money, in Jesuit's Collection boxes?
Ashtar Command at the Alien Residence on Crystal mountain.
World-Bridger not walls;*Crop circles try the Nectar connection.
We never live more than 60 kms. from a camouflaged ley line ~
Can't see monkeys in the photo; I threw the bananas over a fence!
Just live life and see what happens.
*

<u>Global* Tribal* Astral</u>
Acceptance allows the Love to grow ~
Being and Becoming to the next plateau.
"Pain is inevitable ~ suffering is optional"
"Anxiety is a natural part of life not a Negative."
Solar Orbitals in your infinitely free astral space.

An Oyster Broker

"Did I ever tell you 'bout my Heaven and Hell Baby?"
Baba you have taken a Big Hit, needs right energy!
Blocks denying you any pleasure; Pleading, Please,
there's nothing wrong with Joy & Passion is there?
Whether going to the end or finishing earlier.
We keep on Living, we keep on smiling ~
Happy we keep flowing ~ with an Open heart.
You Are that light at the end of this tunnel!
Whatever you agree ~ It's All A Mind Game.
He's bullshitting you, he's burnt the garlic!
Love Is Everything*Loving Consciousness.
Knowing that we are part of Mother Earth.
Peace in our hearts ~ Love knows it's Real.
'She Loves Ice Cream' really crazy, Oh my God!
Do you have a God, somewhere in a cupboard?
Do we need to eat Lobsters really?
Even if you're living there as a tribe
in tune with nature ~ went out onto the reef.
Caught for Crimes Against Intra*Planetary.
The dancer becoming the dance.

*

'CHOICE'

Doin' everythin' by a Clock * Clockin' In Clockin' Off!
Ecstatic Space men snorkeling ~ on a turquoise reef;
Not working in the blistering, back-breaking rice paddies!
I take on this identity that I like, Multi * Dimensional Baba.
Out there exists because of in here ~ A Mental-movement.
You're doing what you like, what feels right ~ in this moment.
Fully dreaming of desire and companionship, not just physical.
Enjoy that instant ~ transcending all the fields of a limited Mind.

'Birth Certificated Fund'
You are who You Are ~ Not really your Name.
Fine dust sifting through our elements ~ time.
To do a journey inside ~ a lot of lights in there.
"You're only a breath away ~ from death Mr. Sufi"
Then that STOPS ~ Taking in Prana, breathing essence.
"I'd like 20 years in Martinique with gorgeous You, Baby"
We live in a myth! Those tears are healing.

*

Gave me a Kiss, the nails and 2 planks of wood!
All frequencies are in the brain ~ fall into it fully Consciously.
On your own journey * Inward is Outward's Magic black box!
Using language to affect our Mind, behavior, understanding,
response. Could you explain Freedom 'Conscious Freedom'?
'Divine even Natural Justice'? ~ 'This is NOT for Everyone!'
'Offer your other cheek for a slap and be made into a Slave'
Satisfaction when you don't need anything ~ It's all 'Object'
formed in Space & we see this illusion as 'REAL REALITY!
Mental-movement. Crucified on a hot summer's afternoon!
"You've had enough but you don't know you've had enough
once you've got this thing in your head, going More, More!"
Frazzled * bedazzled * razzled ~ Changing Your Mind-set.
'It is recommended that our viewers not try this at home!'
These are images that All people should find Outrageous!

*

Kismet's Kiss
There's light after death ~
Surrendering my Heart to Divine Bliss for a kiss.
Real eyes ~ Open feelings, Youniversal Love.
ACCEPTING IT ALL

"If you cut me I bleed"
Time is your master ~ time is a disaster.
Time doesn't exist and intuitive feeling is ~
Her hazel eyes are still twinkling like diamonds.
Moving my destiny as my Palmist said, 'This will also change'
It's about not taking it too personally ~ All temporary Forms.
I'm human ~ I have a heart beating inside this Space suit!
Star crossed lovers ~ passion, guilt, rejection, pain, death.
You're the best analyst but how do you know?
There are no buts, there is no thinking either.

*

Universal Dynamic Holograms
Psychedelic Power Tools not Neo Economic Slavery.
Sharing the Love Creation ~ free Tantric tongues.
Inner light beams * iridescent peacocks dancing.
Diamond heart chakras on Hanuman's beach.
Sacred geometry in organic herbal gardens.
Temptation between Euphoria and Utopia.
Juicy fruit ~ full on trip to a Sun God.

*

Then I Binged Up!
I Got my pension after working in a coffee shop
close to the Psychedelic Museum in Amsterdam!
"I'm an Entheogenic Tourist ~ Not a Terrorist!"
Crimson Violet Visa ~ SPACE for EVERYONE.
"I'm happy looking at the grass not Crackoland!"
Dependent on the people providing the Power.
'Thais plant the rice, Cambodians look after it,
the Laotians listen to it' from morning 'til night.
But I said we're living in sunny Anjuna, Goa!

Prima *Vera* Bliss

'Incredible India if you can put up with a lot of shit you'll like it!'
'Chelo Bhutan' ~ Escaping the System for Real*Psyche Stars.
In a Woman's sex being a Goddess ~ For better or worse we
want the better because when the worst comes they fuck off!
"I always like to be right because I win by making you wrong!"
Clashes of Ego movement all hinges on a Self's-Identity!
Love when you recognize Love in another ~ reflection.
The recognition of Consciousness running through it all.
You are here now but sometimes you are not aware.
Thoughts are always there, you can't own anything.
All Forms have a 'Life-span' coming ~ going, gone
not meant to be permanent, forever & never!

*

My God it's Alive!

Harmonise with nature ~ Planet Earth is our Pearl!
Trees are Oxygen giving life to Humans
Humans reflecting back Consciousness.
It's true if you want to believe it ~
People don't see beyond the 'Object'
Being the 'Subject' of Universal Space.
Here I Am as its expression ~ Gaia Fire Power.
Relating to situations as if it is My life's, 'FORM'
The person you see is an Illusion, Ego, fractal,
A Self Identified Mental-state ~ 'Me in the head!'
Causes all the wars, problems, selfish f… ignorance.
Losing sight of the whole picture, 'Universal Subject'
The key to Life, the Amazing thing is it's Not Me ~
Let the Light Shine through coming from the Still
Space of Unconditional Love.

The Vulva Saga

Eating fresh fica with sweet Eva in a garden of delights.
"I got No fear of rejection, I've worked in Insurance,
no worries being told to Fuck Off!" "FUCK OFF!"
Turn the lights off and the music up to 432 Hz!
Tibetan ringing bowls, Ayahuasceros' healing tones!
'You Live your life or be dragged around by your Mind'
& her expectations reflected in you ~ 'Lover Beware'
Do yu know what I mean about natural harmonics?

*

Obsidian Jet Dynasty

"We're too Intelligent to have a psychosomatic J O B mate!"
They shot themselves in the foot, as they do; Jobs for the boys.
Passion's not very high ~ resistance against being deeply intimate,
in heavenly bliss. I had to wait 'til you turned up at the end for a kiss.
'Men's colony' is a 'Private prison' the 'Plaza' is a Toll booth in US.
'Human condition' What about murderous criminals like Somali pirates?
Don't offer your left over food or they'll tell you to "Fuck Off!"
Adding Insult to Injury And you'll be arrested for it in Florida!
The love of money is like a bad drug You become heartless
Greed kills the Soul, selling out even rainwater to the Devil.

*

Sky Pilot Inspace

Own it, trust your own feelings don't blame anyone else!
Those memories from the past & Future's Imaginations.
Love's Obsession ~ It's from the reflexive Mind.
EGO wants to grab on tight and Possess it ~
when really it needs to let it go ~ in the flow.
Show them a World without Mind-Control.
Don't deny feelings which make us human.
What is the note playing in your heart?
Who I Am!

Eternally IS Quantum

One step higher than being on the lower manifest level ~
Harmonisng more white light for all not holding up FORM.
Struggling in body/mind ~ why fight, jump out and be Free!
Into the flow ~ not holding on, bringing you to the Oceanic.
Taking another drop into Infinite Space * trusting the light.
Define it as you want; Have you got your confidence back?
It's in my hand I didn't want to let the banana bullshit go yet.
You have had that experience ~ resonating within Revelation.
Not to be fanatically Possessed or the game is eating you!
Reflecting who you are eternally.
The Energetic fields.

*

Formless ~ Energy

Egoist Fully Selfish-Identified Mental-State.
Awareness is what we call knowing 'Nothing'
It's too simple for the complicated Mind to get ~
You can't know it Mentally or understand with Mind.
Let's talk about the 'Delusional Objective' in Space ~
It's not as it seems, the Artificial-Self, Me, this Person.
Which is called 'Separation' ~ this is Mine, that's Yours!
The Space * Is the Ultimate State Not the 'Object' in it ~
Getting it, losing it, being at ease with its impermanence.
Knowing it will disappear ~ not arguing with any moment.

*

Fixing!

Planet Earth
Is an Addiction Colony
The human species In Space

*

Lovey * Dovey

"I haven't been in the Program"
Can't you just be you?
Shake your dreads!

Tumor cells committing suicide!
Hanging over an egg up my arse ~ now you are free to fly!
Broken shells, forget it! In the real world you can believe in
the egg and you won't break out of the egg; It has to break!
Holding onto our old descriptions for the same blessings…
You get your mind as a friend to work with you
Not being confined with right or wrong.
All is the expression of the heart.
Inside changing perceptions ~
unraveling LOVE definitions.
"Her eyes are open"

*

WHAT IS A REVOLUTION?

"We keep killing insurgents but they keep on f…g coming back!"
Appalling loss of human life, one of the great disasters of War!
Jesus carrying a sheep. Anarchists ~ Assassinated by the Army
or simple, humble doctrine, eyes staring in amazement into Infinity.
Symbolism of Power, Tyrants wearing purple brocaded Imperial togas.
Mothership Extra terrestrial figures hugging each other to help uplift us all.
"Cambodian Bling, except that it's from Sweatshop Economics in China!"

*

'Gaza Concentration Camp'
They used to want Headlines on every 24/7 media channel ~streaming LIVE!
Now have you noticed that since the US wars in Iraq and Afghanistan and
especially since the Arab spring Revolutions throughout the Middle East
there's no News on the plight of their hated neighbor Israel, aka Holy Land!
With a spokesperson from the Knesset or Mossad cajoling for understanding
when their drone's just destroyed a Palestinian school! They don't want
to distract anybody from their view that Arabs are annihilating each other
and Zionists are somehow good guys! The more people are suppressed
the bigger the Revolution! Rules & Regs. for Absolutely everything,
it's like that right?

Gift towards Atrocity!

Killing another 3 year old terrorist from the 'Genocide Kindergarten!'
Another sacrificial lamb to slaughter ~ what yur thinking of Abraham?
US Donated jet fighters, $20 billion 'Military Aid' 2nd biggest fleet of F16's!
Does it say in the Torah about Israel; Racist, State supported Apartheid?
Whose Fascist fiefdom is this Baron? Ask any Satanic NEOCON. demon.
Who are their Idols worshipping? Just look at the results and ask yourself!

*

Einstein's E*Space

Looking into the Perfect Picture ~
Pops a mirror out as a natural rebirthing.
'All geometry is Sacred geometry ~
"It's the bag that tells the story!"
How am I supposed to stop a runaway donkey?
It's the Meaning, intent, that you bring to the Temple.
What energy you carry in your heart ~ transformational.
Not better or worse duality, they need us around too.
Weaving us into the Separation ~ it's all Mental-Illusion.
Astral Channeling * Conceptions of a Crystal mandala.
Shiva Valley brings it out*Everything is Formless Space.
"You can't have one without the other"
"You can bring Fear anywhere."
"No need for that reaction dear!"
"I don't have that sensation ~"
"Others feeling as much as you!"

*

Purgatory

Another Massacre in the name of God!
Cardinal Sinners under a scarlet dome.
Burning heretics live at the Holy stake.
The punishment of deviant Theo Crazy.
Megalomaniac Popes on the rampage!

COSMIC YONI

Mind constantly Bombarding your heart with de*illusions ~
We want to fill in the Space*Program which is Conditioned!
Money buys you time ~ "I have a soft spot for Smart Robots"
"They want people living in Fear so they can keep the lid on them!"
All being programmed with the same super conductor Marvel chip,
telling us they're hungry, sleeping or when they're not in the mood.
"If you think the economy is more important than the environment
try holding your breath while counting your money." G Mc Pherson.
"Doesn't anyone believe in 'Live and Let Live' anymore?"
Sucking it all up!

*

"I couldn't even get a job when there were jobs!"

Intriguing, Queen ordered Papists, Hung, drawn and quartered!
Any Jesuits controlling the drug trade in Columbia? Ask the CIA!
Welcome to the Anti-Christ Centre; Operating their God's will!
Raising up the revolution then letting it fail; What's the effect?
Power > Who owns the Federal Reserve? Who funds the NSA?
Ask the Knights of Malta, Knights of Columbus, Secreta Monita.
Who is the Intelligence arm of the Vatican; CIA controlling USA?
Global Politics wants to restore the Temporal Power of the Pope!

*

Ashamed of Humanity

'God has no religion' ~ Mahatma Gandhi.
'Invited to a haunting Public Execution ~
Not legitimizing murder in any way!'
A courageous heart being an 'Objective' War photographer.
'Screaming in his eyes ~ No shortage of human flesh.
Throwing a grenade, bringing death to others'
"Daddy was a victim of war's insane vibration ~"
Don Mc Cullin, (BBC 2 July 2013)

<u>Pentagon in situ</u>
Resident ET hybrid heritage ~
"Not all Reptilians are bad Aliens."
"We're all here to serve a purpose."
Took away their Consciousnesses.
They gave her a gift of their tears!
A little child sitting in the Torture cell,
more ritually sacrificed in the Holy sea.
$3^{rd\ D.}$ density Cabals in control of Society.
Development of the 4th Reich; 'Macts frei!'

*

<u>When your dreams get Shattered!</u>
You told her the truth and the truth can hurt!
When you get to where I am and feel what I feel
You will realise what an Unconscious, Ignorant monster you were.
Intentions take you out of the flow, Space has no definition, no END
that's why Mind can't get it! How to switch OFF Addicted Attachments?
I know how to do that ~ Spiritual Alchemy

*

<u>This Is Chemical</u>
On line Gurus witnessing the Consciousness
Beyond Consciousness ~ the Knower of ultimate Brahm.
"When the identity of the body dies what's left is Absolute"
"When the Power of Love overcomes the Love of
Power the World will know Peace." Jimi Hendrix.
Are the stressful Starfish * friendly in Djibouti?
You need a spear gun ~ You need a bit of Love!

*

<u>Solar Star</u>
Enjoy the day
And night in flight
Embrace the morning light
Smile at the moon in your dreams

Not from Things that never last

Julia Klitskyhigher at Leninskinova's Juice Bar, Morjim.
'Wanted' ~ Pink holes Geishas who'll Love to fuck me!
Full, Possessed by dark spiritual Forces ~ Unconsciously.
Identifying with activities ~ only their own Super Ego entity!
Primary role or Fear with desire, human beings Caste rated.
No more reactions ~ all melting into One heavenly vibration.
Being happy by knowing who you are, existing in Primal Space.
Be Conscious don't accumulate doom and gloom ~ Spirit of Life.
Put your treasure in the Space of Awareness ~ beyond y/our Mind.
Not having A Mental-Form Control enslaving thoughts in y/our head!
No problems with Possession; No separation then everything is y/ours.
Making Puja on her roof, full of Jasmine with an angel who is a muse.
Suffering Primates in cages it's horribly true; Freed Love is the answer.
When will you learn to let her go? Accepting she's chosen another life!

*

Neonicotinoids Photopanicon

In the multi*dimensional Garden of Eden.
Brain damaged Honey Bees ~ All in One!
Can't pollinate 75% of the World's crops.
Lost in space ~ 85% reduction of Queens.
When Pacifying Maniacal, Manic anarchy!
Close Gitmo to the Neutralino Krill mystery.
And finally protecting Sea Horses of Islands
in flowing Ocean jet streams ~ Shakti Bhakti.
Divine eyes full of Bliss.

*

3 in us

You don't forgive anybody.
You forgive Yourself ~
for suffering from it

Angel Star Power
Everything is nothing ~ You going with the flow.
Magical Crystal Love touch of Samantabhadra.
The Consciousness you give to delusions from Venus.
*Melting demons with our Love ~ All Mind * One Mind.*
"Are you a Slave, switched on?" 'Yes You!'
Love frequency in Unconditional Space.
Liberation from the Suffering Identity ~
Feeling Silence ~ Soothing Stillness.
Realising You are it already, Aloha!
Entranced harmony ~ Has No Fear.

*

Kali * Fatwa!
In a charred field of broken hearts!
A Fiction of Separation ~ Telepathy
*You & me * Baby!*
"I was getting it wasn't you?"
Enjoy what you can, you never know
when the next twinkling one is coming.
'In the moment ~ I'm off the hook'
Something fundamentally to do!

*

Devil's Real Time
A Theatre of War developed into ONE MORE Human Tragedy!
Another suicide attack on a Mosque during Friday prayers!
Downloading Incendiary & Fragmentation Cluster Bombs!
"AND NEVER FORGET WHAT HAPPENED IN BIAFRA"
'1000 dying children in front of you; They wanted food!
Two year olds crawling around on their stomachs.
Blind and Insane; So horrible it couldn't be real!
What dignity they had, inches away from death!'
"Today I am feeling Reborn"

Liberty Sale
We don't know how to let go
because all these things
make me who I am ~ habitual ID.
We think we are the experience....
We're not ~ "I came in a rainstorm"
You weren't there, figuring your future.
Lost hope ~
She gave up!
Ask for the light
to be turned on!
In through the Crown
turn on the Sun beam ~
Reflecting Divine for Confirmation.

*

'Subject' ~ Grace in Space
They see themselves as being put here by the Universe.
Identification of another Mind-concept is not
the discovery of Real Intelligence Inside us.
There is No Good or Bad it's just 'Thinking' ~
Same Intelligence saying it's not really True!
All is Space in the Absence of thou ......ght.
Surrendering to the Suffering is release,
transcends existential games of 'Illusion'
Taking it out of the Ego realm ~
Coming out of the Cosmic Egg.
With the delusion there is Us
not seeing beyond 'Object'.

'Nothingness is Best'
Then you're out of trouble.
Mind is an imaginative Creator ~
The Eternal Truth is not for Sale.
She said, 'just play with me'
"If the Magic is not there
You can let her go!"
Fall in Love ~
or grow in Love
Spreading ~ being the light.
In winter's frozen fields of fear.
Being the Love all the time.
When you crash
You need somewhere there
The Light is Free

*

Flying High
I'm as a King of the Galaxy ~ Free to flow
You are the woman who took me to the Sun and Moon
And went with me to the most twinkling Stars in Heaven.

*

Nihilistic Cymbals
When we first met you said I would break your heart ~
Not if you broke my heart first with SHOCKING Surprise!
Listen to the music in the telepathy between you and me.
Tell me what's blocking you from jumping into my arms ~
I need to know the truth of why your heart's changed feelings.
Seeing the light with me my gracious, glorious sweet heart.

Tesla's Clairvoyance

"Forgive them of course they don't know what they're f.....g doing!"
"Fanatical devotion to exalted ideals of National egoism and Pride
is prone to plunge the World into Primitive Barbarism and strife."
You are frightened to commit again ~ It's a Gandhiji Operation.
You are right, who ever really knows what will happen?
'PRISM' 'TEMPORA' 'Boundless Informant' Programs.
NSA, CIA, GCHQ; HARVESTING Trillions of data packets.
Unjustified trawling Your emails, SKYPE, phone calls, intimate foreplay.
Everything Recorded in case we find a naughty, gossiping Terrorist cell!
Governmental Excuses compounded; Guilty of stealing all your Privacy.
Spin doctors exhumed to spin the blame onto the messengers of Truth.
They'd rather spend their money on looking for water on distant Mars!
Free Range eggs exposed to radiation. The Anti Anti Anti Missile!
"They're all good flights until they fall out of the sky!"
I'd like to know what happened to him; Standing in front of a fully
Tooled up Tank in Tiananmen Square! So does everybody else...
Spiritual music ~ they've seen what it's all about.
Anything happens head straight out to sea ~
Turn right at the Tigris outside of Babylon!
By-passing radioactive, poisoned Fukushima!

*

Astral * Projections

I'm havin' a burnout ~
see you in a few weeks!
Incessant complaining, negativity, fearful.
Looking into your eyes, all you got to know.
They will wait because they want it!
Mastery of the Mind-sets ~ Proactive*Properties.
I Am so fabulous ~ Being tuned into the Cosmos!
Reflecting ourselves in the Higher Consciousness.
Focusing on delight, everybody's happy.

31

Cosmo * Naught

You're bringing back messages from Inner galaxies!
Flying high * In *Outer * Quantum Space.
Accepting & Understanding
Everything Is Possible ~
Sweet dreams Baby.

*

Her Melting Bush

"Oh fuck, Yeah Baby!" "You are the Love you are searching for!"
Walking in summer meadows of brilliantly shining buttercups.
'It is what it is' * Erotic Cosmic * in the Tantric Love Temple!
'Free access to local sluts site' ~ Don't you love humanity!?
Nothing to be frightened of until you get closer to the edge ~
Gathering up the people and dropping them on their heads!
A Zen joke, Cinderella with Tourettes; Still in deep SHOCK!
He was a Happy Bunny, still the shantiest guy in town!
'Save the Fluffy Pussy Party' I wanna be in that one.
Then it is just Celebration of Life isn't it?

*

Non-Prophit

The Animation of Infinity ~
Channeling of the moment.
Making a commitment to a cow!
I want a place with No Paranoia,
Rites & Rituals ~ different Illusions.
"They made it cost so much that people
have to work all their lives to pay the electric bill!"
Shows how that Power takes the human from the human.
He was tempted! He was facing Kali's Skull Shrine Baba
And that's not a pretty picture.

Yogic *Logic* Vedantic *Pedantic
"India produces a lot of Graduates Baba!"
Eastern Philosophy with western concepts...
Still in SHOCK! ~ Being Cosmic fusion on a happy plasma wave.
What happened to the tender loving care darling ~ evaporated!
Up to each of us to live our PEACE for the good of all. TRYING!
They're living with no stimulation, no epiphany, still no revelation.
Why suffer with unrequited desire, envy ~ Move to the Himalayas.
*Don't want a Starfish * One leg in the air staring at the sky!*
*Existential Cosmic Molecules *** Soul to Soul Connectivity*
"Stay in the cool shade!"
_*_

Dutch girls riding bikes
I've been holding on to this image that I couldn't ever let go.
Too precious, couldn't imagine letting contentment flow ~ off!
I like it, I love it, I want to keep it, never wanna lose that vibe!
Full Passionate addiction, squirt me another endorphin fix ~
from your delicious, lascivious spirit's mix of intoxicating delights
desires and raging fires for my Mind to conjure up and recreate!
But it's all been a very beautiful and tragic delusional dream ~
Next one is different; I seem to be in another place of the Spiral.
You have to let it go because there's Nothing left to hold onto but
her ghost. There comes that moment in time, its changed ~ Gone!
Have to let it go, she's fucked off; Holding on is what she's left you
at most! It's impossible to carry on, change has naturally come to
set me, to set us free, to be at peace, releasing the addict, finding
a new reality of higher consciousness & Unconditional Love Space!
Great now take it easy, get your senses back
and tune into the blossoming Lotus heart.

"I want to look into your deep blue eyes!"
Love and Light downpouring ~ erotic rainbows.
Licking full passion, melting on my Goddess' lips.
Penetration deep into her steaming rain forest.
I want to seduce your hard throbbing nipples,
I want to suck your honey sweet sensual clit.
I want to touch the fire in your gorgeous arse.
I want to kiss your erogenous nymphs from Venus
dancing on the tip of your wild ~ delirious tongue.
I want to cum inside you like two exploding stars.
I want to feel you sliding up my hard cock in ecstasy,
screaming, unbridled in never ending exquisite rapture.
I want to hold your true love tightly in my arms.
I want to taste and smell your wet multi*orgasms.
You aren't going anywhere and I want to be
forever inside you in such beautiful bliss.
Letting our love reunite ~ reignite in us!
Your open heart has declared its love for me.
I want to ravish your sublime, dripping pussy,
devour it as a delicious Sicilian cheesecake.
My fingers pressing into your sacred Temple,
my body's desire to caress its burning flame.
I want to embrace your free spirit ~ with mine.
I want to lie beside you in Heaven's tranquility
My magma flowing into your Divine ~ Oceanic

*

"I do" ~ "I do"
Inspired so in tune with each other.
You're letting her go free ~ to choose herself.
And she decided to fuck off without a word!
A step up and really hard thing to do.
Tuning up ~ words feeling strong Magic.

** Bhakti Trans*mission Tower **
Spontaneous Coup de foudre * with Bliss * full Shakti
Impossible to predict what her Mind will do, look at you!
Enjoying sublime Ecstasy under a sacred Banyan tree.
Telepathy is Acceptance ~
being Open ~ Smiling Inside
To Give & to receive ~ Life's Celebration.
Create your Heart Paradise
*

What Are Your Rights?
"Law abiding citizens have nothing to fear
except from their lying, criminal governments."
"If I have to come over here again there'll be
lots of red dots appearing all over your body."
Automatic fire ~ Rock and Roll button off! On! Off!
Realising we are all Cosmic Space manifesting; On!
Where is the simple humanity of Liberty, generosity?
Feeling the magical passion inside our Space suits.
Enjoying life to the MAX ~ in gratitude, humility.
Being Inspiration * Being Love.
*

The Bioenergetics Dream
Flying out from under Paranoia.
Dropping your liquid thoughts ~
The day dream ~ the night dream
Another LeVeL of Consciousness.
Manifesting Life * Manifesting Love
All you gotta do is breathe loving ~
breathe it in ~ exhale it out to OM.
Letting your Goddess go ~ into Space.
Love is shining * we're all Sufis inside.
Your direct connection.

DESIRE*ENVY

Free Expression ~ No rules in the Galaxy Capt. Inspiration!
Utopian thoughts blowing out of a peace Pipe." "Cannabis
produces dopamine connections between neural pathways"
"Self esteem Ego, covers self worth, covers the Real worth"*
"Don't know if it's good until we try it, what good will come"
"Person centred therapy ~ journey of being and becoming"
Primed ~ how will we ever know our fully conscious mind?
Everything is a reflection of Inside ~ Our own Cosmos.
*"I think therefore I am not" * Astral orbs in your eyes**
I think where forth I'm nothingness in Infinite Space

*

Reality Caravanserai

You need some form of light in the Centre of the sacred Yoni.
Keep away from me with Your fear, deceit and Selfish confusion!
After a year of stress, running away from me for your own needs.
My complete rejection and denial ~ Your craving to love the next.
Dumped, paralysed in empty space, lets me drown alone in memories!
"Now only come to me with smiles & love ~
feelings in your heart to give fully to me."
Instead You asked me for help to rescue you again!
Any Understanding It's beyond comprehension
just be here now in the Magic ~ together or not!
'New new' ~ Letting go of your knowledge
basking in an Ocean of Chaos ~ Infinite drops.
Try making heads or tails of it ~ Living it instead.
What are you really saying you want to give
and what are you truly wanting from me?
I remember your joy the first days we met.
Look into the mirror and ask yourself….
Why would I hate you?

Perfection*Perception PROJECTION *ERECTION
Deep Slit / Perspective, if you got the balls ~ Ping the Clit!
I will always treasure this expression of the deepest feelings
of your heart. How far this sexy angel quickly fell from grace!
'All she wants, Primal Penis, can't fuck without Shiva's ling!'
Women love to give blow jobs; Waking up the Love Cock.
"Pain is inevitable ~ Suffering is optional" same position,
different passion; Psychedelic trippers v Egoistic schemers.
With Consciousness & Inspiration otherwise we destroy the
ones we Love & ourselves from fearful, self-centred Ignorance.
Sustaining the highest levels of Devotion as a human ~ being.
Can you even imagine my feelings, the suffering on the inside!

*

Eternity * Infinity
'Experience your life not IMAGINING FEAR of DMZ death'
Who remembers Wounded Knee anymore? Mai Lai Fuk?
Government Policy, Police for Peace, No Power to people!
Civil War as usual, exploitation as usual, Ignorance as usual!
'Just given a job to do General, massacre all those darn Injuns!'
USA genocide in Vietnam, who's still alive; Remember that one?
Let's have another 'Free Fire Zone' losing All Hearts & Minds
and all the bloody rest! Using demons to get what you wanted!
"Don't torture yourself anymore!"

*

'Nature of Solar Space'
"Tu peut attraper mon Robot stp?"
Cybernetic Tortoise chasing red crystal light waves ~
Venus in your Mind, in your heart, kissing your Spirit's moist lips ~
Reading the 'Pyschedelic Prophet' poetry in a sunlit Sufi Rose garden.
With dying breath, your last thought, 'how much will be the death tax duties?'
Capitalist Philosophy, Your Insane memorial to Entheogens of Ego & greed!
Inspiring all the Angels to come back into the Sunlight

*<u>Wakey Wakey * DIY Anarchy!</u>*
Imagine if your wife was called Venus Paradise!
A hippy from Universo Parallelo ~ It's Real Fire!
Conforming more to Insanity, the fascist Society.
A Criminalised Justice Bill or the Big Foot tool?
*They want to be FREE * FREE Be Who You Are.*
Peace Convoy Activism ~ Go and have a Party!
Feeding time ~ It happens by Itself.
'Trespassers Will Be Executed'
Where's the Hope for the future?
Exhilarating people's experience.
*

<u>Ego Perfuming the Ether</u>
Don't pull Dandelions, need 'em for the bees!
"You can't let go of something
If you don't know what it is."
It's about letting it all go ~ Interstellar.
*STOP *Silence *Stillness *Observe*
The 'I' Hologram lighting up
My Identity ~ Sense of Self haiku.
That's what the brain constructs
filtering 40,000,000 signals per sec!
Developing a 'Reality' we can accept.
*All is in the Heart * Soul's Love Space*
*

<u>Watch this Gap</u>
'It's the Space that's more essential than what's in the Space'
Take it to the MAX then drop it when you've peaked!
*Chemical Parties*You don't wanna do that! Why not?*
Music Is Fusion if my heart can take it.
Be on the limit ~Give it Totality
Then let go ~ rhythm flowing now

<u>Caught Psyche*phrenic</u>
"I'm in a spider's web." * *Is this really the best you can do?*
An open chakra all over the place ~ only if you want to be.
As one heart of Love r*evolving through the infinite Cosmos
Being in bliss same sensitivity frequency ~ intense Memories*
Wiped clean Baby, remember what it is to have feelings?
Ready for Spaciousness ~ it's our different awareness!
'Life after death an adventure into nothingness'

*

<u>Don't Forget What's that about ~ Again?</u>
When she left in the middle of the night ...tip toe
I never wanted to wake up ~ being together lost in Love.
She's blocked our telepathic resonance ~ contact dropped.
Why? Always try to be honest & clear, no misunderstanding,
no disconnection nor Rejection, have self-respect & self-Love.
Being open going deep ~ way into our heart, don't you know?
She gave up! Betrayal, denial, switched Feelings off all together!
Walking along the shore of Broken Hearted Dreams ~ Remember
You Are the Love.

*

<u>Endo*Cannabinoid System</u>
Brainwashed about Miraculous Marie Jane.
"There is no profit in being a healthy society"
Magic Balls, Igm. a day keeps Illness away!
Just say 'No' to Alcohol ~ A gateway to 'war on drugs!'
Heroin for your cough dear? Rather have a Psycheactive!
"Just takes the edge off things" ~ "He's holding a fat joint!"
Anti Inflammatory ~ they prescribed Toxic poison not CBD!
Cannabis THC. eats Cancer cells! Get it Online from Holland.
"I'll be your sunshine all morning and everything at night"
"You made me understand Love" ~ "I'll make you Satisfied!"

Amsterdam Canals

"The crowd didn't want it anymore, a crazy war on Cannabis!"
Couldn't believe it buying Mary Jane at the coffee counter
without a care in the World; None of the usual Paranoias!
Real Haze Shock ~ Waking up with her again in my brain!
In my mind's territory, each morning, in my heart's memory
can't seem to ever let her go ~ until Now, Now, Now, Now.

*

Planete * Comete #8

*Integrational * Telepathy*
"Turn the radiators down!"
*Tao Haiku * 'Love is greater*
than any one ~'

*

To go to Mars * to Know the Universe

Do you want to buy property in Vegas, on Venus, cheap?
We demand to know if it's GMO or anything else unnatural!
Scientists have found*Rosemary increases Memory X7.
Yantra maps to other Solar systems, turn right at Niburu.
*Ghandava's gravity * Programmed by the Astral*Cosmos.*
Let's cherish Pachamama before heading to outer Space.

*

1st Priority: Human Not their Role

I read the autobiography of an Organic yoghurt pot.
A very interesting story about absolutely f…. nothing.
Did you ever feel devoured by black Kali's Avengers?
Galloping elephants charging through your Lotus heart!
Slaughter House, he should go and work in an Agarbati shop.
And She wore Parvati's Rose petals between her lips ~
Let's all go to the Valley of Flowers

Cellular Thought

Two little fish trying to find the river ~
You can Know things without Knowing.
Mind's Illusion of making us Think we Know.
Why do we believe it; Forms Made in Space?
"If you feel that you have something to defend
Know that you have identified with an Illusion.
Suffering the emotional Pain of the Ego!" Ask God!
Nervous breakdown, devastated, old concepts falling apart.
"Most people live in dumb down Mediocrity * is there something more?"
Reaffirming our Identity, hypnotized by their own environmental mirage.
Addictions dreaming nothing better, "I think you are my Honey Quean!"
What thoughts can do to us, "You became Possessed by a demon darling!"
Was it improper protein production, hormones, nutrients, neural peptides,
desensitized, deregulated, signals from the brain, internal juices of desire?
Addicted to your receptors ~ eyes searching for a certain Emotional state.
Detaching the 'I know what you need' drug from a muse on fire!

*

Your Third Eye

True ~ Love cannot be Imagined with the Mind!
Creating your own Universe ~ how You like it and You
can 'In create' it also* the Unexpected has to be there.
It's not visible but in this moment ~ It is experienced
in a way you'll recognize it * You Make its expression
Real then You Are It ~ in your imagination & aura fields.
It's always changing ~ Levels of high frequency to Perfect!
Telepathy sharing y/our feelings' * Loving Consciousness.
Behave like Knights in shining Armor or at least not like f....
stupid, perverted morons, brothers! And sisters stand in
Your Goddess' light and let's all shine on together.
Knowing You are part of Mother Earth ~
Love is everything * Peace in our Hearts

41

Swimming Together

As Original as a Super Blue Elf Association can get!
Seeing it, the abstraction * You must see it! Traffic ~
Pile-up! Outside Aishwarya's ~ on the same bend!
'He just went and lived with the Lions ~
He knew a couple of Lionesses there…..
Accepted as part of the pride, creating bonds.
'They are wild animals but they're not beasts!'
'The cathartic effect.'

*

Space of the Holy Cow

Just Looking Not Acting ~
Judging this other as 'I AM'
Listening to the sound of Silence.
Realising It Is with Your Full Attention!
Who's banning your idiosyncratic taboos?
Need a beer, pork chop and a rare Mumbai Steak!
I can remember getting speed pills for a thrupenny bit.
5 bob on drugs and out all night ~ The freedom to be me!

*

Sutra * 000'

An Open Secret, they're all Masons ~ Jesuit fingers in the gelati!
People who kill people I don't know what it ever truly solves!
Can buy a rifle at ASDA; They don't burn lepers in Benares.
People Identify with the contents ~ 'Objects' of their Minds!
Not the Live Space of it.

*

Trippy in Primrose

"It's not a Bar it's a Psychedelic Temple Inside!"
Reclaiming all the resonances of the Planet
for the People of the Planet.

History is full of Revolutions!
Being here now simple Awareness, Consciousness comes through you.
Not knowing where it comes from ~ I feel a Live channel opening up.
No War, 'Smokin' Chillums on the Beach in front of Shiva's place.'
They're making all the decisions for themselves!
"I'm a Sun worshipper when I get up"
'I do Love me for who I Am in Space'
We have Resistance * Venus is too hot!
She's been banned from the Punjab.
Withdrawal ~ fuck off it's a drug!
Coming down from Love.
*

Innocent Perception
Greatness doesn't come from anything you Know....
It's coming from that Creative Space Inside each of us ~
It's not what you do it's how you do it * Innermost energy.
Happy you don't know, can't know it's all mental Projection.
Conscious * Awareness Seeing your Essence * in Love ~
Love is in all things. 'The Real Reality' ~ our natural state,
no Conditionings. Love is your Perception, no boundaries,
no more Identity. I can LOVE whatever I'm perceiving not
projecting EGO. Then you feel it in your Heart ~ THIS IS
ALL ME * LOVE for ALL LIFE ~ Spiritual transformation.
*

Eating Venus' Pink Lotus Petals
We're all f... Sufis and they're deluxe hippies from an Ashram!
"I slept like a dead forest" Heart melting stars in deep space.
"I love Monet and Rimbaud but that was donkey's years ago!"
We all get our visions from different places, inter-connection.
The magic is flowing down a ley line and you're in my arms.
Breathing bliss into the Cosmic Gulf-stream.

<u>At this Moment...</u>
She's a forest fairy he's a Priapic pixie not a deranged blue elf.
Great to have a super muse, romantic geisha no Demon Ego!
No Self, no Id of Sense; No suffering, no dramatic Queens.
No Mental-Form making Me, Mine, thine & any other sign.
All you can do really is accept what you are feeling inside.
Bringing that into the light of Conscious acceptance ~
Knowing the Power that's in line with what's happening.
No limitations ~ of indefinable 'Me' 'I' so why define it?
The Goddesses' Temple in wild, freest pink pulsations!
Everyone's a winner ~ Not putting resistances to Life.
*

<u>'No Fear They're Free'</u>
Carrying on at 'Cafe del Sol' in a desert Oasis.
Opening her petals of an Egyptian blue Lotus,
see what happens ~ Saying Yes to raw food!
Green, red, yellow, black, white all illusionary.
Dark mystic gypsy, sultry bohemian fairy.
"I wouldn't be good on a slave ship!"
Valued only by their price in money!
*

<u>Contradiction of a Paradox</u>
All this brain worshipping and they're just sexy cartoons.
"If you manufacture weapons you don't believe in Peace!"
Cosmonauts in Love, Adam and Eve. How do you respond?
Obviously you're not Interested to ever see me again! Why?
Giving her what she wanted, meeting another new boyfriend.
Special Predator! Treating him like a slave, gaining control!
Suckling energy out of you with no empathy like a vampire.
Life * Light Feeling Inside us all ~ & I got the perfect Magic.

<u>Unconscious < Ironic > Sublimation</u>
*I Love you as a state of reality * an art energy field.*
"And I love Tarantulas ~ they like their stomachs tickled"
She told me about 'loyalty' to her new man as she twisted
the dagger of betrayal and rejection into her Lover's heart!
"If you're looking for that one special person who can
change your life take a look into the mirror of your Soul!"
'Kindness in words creates kindness, kindness in thinking
creates profoundness, kindness in giving creates Love.' Lao Tzu.
You left me without a word and are living a life of emotional denial.
You were honest Baba you followed your heart's deepest feelings.
*

<u>Ramana Maharshi * Talk 164</u>
"The Ego is the root of all diseases; Give it up."
Who is it who gives it up? 'Mind the Step, feel the Space.'
"Let come what comes let go what goes ~ see what remains"
Conditioning Programming – Heavy Metal that's like Buddha to him.
A Sufi sentence ~ Super natural, more ecstatic psychic Farsi koans.
Do you know the difference between a Missile & being stoned?
Diving into life's ~ death's ~ life's kundalini omnipresent Ocean.
*

<u>Divine Loving</u>
With an Angel on Top.
Celebrate ~ the day you meet your maker!
Another eye in the heart ~ sees the Invisible.
Living the music through human interaction ~
Sufi healing, Love not fundamental Puritanism.
"You made me understand Love"~ She left me go.
'Her freely willing vibration is being here in Spirit'
How to keep realising Consciousness without her,
*to see another Sun * rise in your devastated heart!*
'She sends Shivas up my spine!'

<u>Something in common deep in the bubbling crucible</u>
She's a holiday hot Robot, lingham*yoni melting together.
Drop dead gorgeous ~ getting that feeling back!
Baby * they know what a hard nipple is!
Wanting to go right back into the womb.
The Mental Identification of temporary
'Things as Real' ~ So we're Suffering!
So Conditioned to the 'FORMulation'
Missing the Space * in our dissociation.
Mr. Dimensional filled with Id. Content.
"When you walk through the forest ~
You don't need to know your name"
*

<u>Goliath at the Door!</u>
'The will of the people shall be the basis of Government authority'
Article 21(3), Universal Declaration of Human Rights.
If someone blows up your whole town and family
You can't ignore it... Can You? So what to do?
On Mazel Tov, Kosher Slaughter House Street.
"US jets and drones flying around the clock!"
Qatar Gas pipes under frackmented Earth.
Boots on the ground... WTF was that!
Transporting the blood of the Planet
to a refinery * Create y/our Paradise.
Oh dear she's gonna do it again!
Our anointed oil ~ burning
Mother Earth up in flames!
A Whirling Sufi Sun dance.
"Where is our Kali?"
The Wrecking Ball.
Heads Rolling!

Putting more sparklers
The frequency of her beating heart ~
"Everything is out there, really it's Inside"
So many different people on the Planet.
You can become a Sannayasin Online!
"You breathe in Peace you exhale Love"
Fiesta & Siesta ~ No Mind on Acid!
Spinning Psychedelic Atomic Balls.

*

Ask the Annunaki * Archons!

Instigating Genocidal killing lust of World Wars or any wars!
Vampires need millions of humans dead as blood sacrifices!
"If you're Conquered you're Conquered ~ what else to do?"
Being a Soul going into Forgiving it all! All to do with having
Human feelings; Lost the empathy, who has any Love left?
Who has cut our DNA strands to make us all their SLAVES?
Learning to step out of the Material game; They want Gold!
Generations going from loving hippies to half dead Zombies!
Brainwashing the great public with their 'Tel a lie vision' World.
Fitting us into their Programming, manufacturing all consent.
Mind-Controlling in all their Channeling, ask Herr. Goebbels.
*Going from Animal Farm to Divine wo/man*Celestial Navigating*
between the 3rd to 5th dimensions of Unconditional Lovingness.
*Mother Earth is a living being * giving every bird a nest.*
*Feeling the Sunshine * Gaia in natural Cosmic order.*
They've Surrendered to the Galactic Federation.
*I want my whole DNA * Consciousness back!*

*

Subjected to the 13 Richest families in the World

'Rothschild, Bruce, Cavendish (Kennedy), De Medici, Hanover,
Hapsburg, Krupp, Plantagenet, Rockefeller, Romanov, Sinclair,
Warburg, Windsor (Saxe-Coburg-Gothe)'. Old & New Oligarchy!

<u>With common sense all is fine</u>
* Multi*verses * a fractal in everybody from that *
don't have the concept of dying in your framework.
Have instead the concept of Knowing ~ Immortality.
This body isn't who You Are, it's just your Space Suit.
Earth is Aligned to another Universe & another one!
Feeling a hot Central Sun beam shining on my face.
Nothing like the angry Scorn of a fully Narcissistic Goddess!
"You can have it all if you are Happy with Nothing!"
Egoless in Gaza! "I don't want any negativity in my heart"

*

<u>Devotional Diva</u>
Yoni worshipping,*clitoris' climax*are you loving a Narcissist?
I thought you'd come back and tell me you loved me forever.
Switching Love on switching it off dumped me, becoming crazy!
Walked into my life, ~ walked out of my life, left me full of pain
Couldn't hold it up, your life was full negativities, anger, stress
A big mess using me to give you meaning, stealing all my bliss.
The Ultra human dream, the Ultimate Love.
Know how to vibrate with it ~ in harmony.
Realising their Intuition of the Cycles ~
turning it on, seeing through the veils.
Accept the switch ~ Quantum Telepathy.

*

<u>In La kech You can realise that You are It.</u>
'The human Mind always needs to Know ~
that's why it Never knows Silence * Space.
"I see you ~ You see me & there Is Life"
Any other Life Form you will give it Love.
Same energy ~ Inner feeling, You.
Don't need to look for what you are.
There Is No path ~ Don't 'Do' Meditation!

Before the Cock Crows

Brilliant*psychology about suffering, tortured enslavement.
Often the victim's chair is on a steel chain bolted to the floor!
Om Shanti Stonehenge, living next to the Army Firing range.
LOVE IS * ULTIMATELY * TRUSTING ~ YOURSELF.
Lucky to have an immune cell left, she's remarried!
No fear, anxiety, stress, doubt, negativity, paranoia!
Left me with an Ultimatum, fulfill my dreams or fuck off!
I got the contract and contacts; I'll cut the Daisy chains,
being in the vibration ~ what is the true meaning of life?
Miracle of light that's why you live in the quantum moment.
It's only a cup & saucer 'Object' spinning in Formless Space.
Yucatan oscillating psychedelic Mayan's on 'nikte'ha' plant trips.
At Chichen Itza sitting on a Pyramid's Apex at first light of Dawn.

*

2nd Cuming in a Mind ~ Stream

Big tits, hot ass, rub my wet pussy, "I like it, I keep it"
Performing my favourite addictions at Dionysus' orgy.
Transcending having the Presence in this unique moment.
Fuckin' talkin' to myself all the time ~ who is in my brain?
Ultimate delusion something you think you love so much!
Not having conditioned thoughts predominate in our head.
"I love the next day after tripping" *Sees the hallucinations!
Look for my True Self, you either are or you're not * All of it.
Not thinking of the future leave it to the Universe to Inspire.
Your part is to give pleasure & let the Celestial give it back.
We're supranatural holograms living now ~ Inner Freedom.
So true ~ Acid trip is in the moment if you get caught in
your thoughts you're fucked! Psychedelic surrealism*
How natural is natural? Love is what you are.
Peace of Mind & Inner Peace in your heart
then wherever you are is Paradise

FORGIVE'

No judging let it be just as it is ~ Amazing because * IT IS *
Sends LIGHT Rays and colours for an ENERGETIC healing.
Emoto's liquid crystal patterns * Sacred vibrational Geometry.
Transcending having the Attention in this present ~ harmony.
You surrender to Consciousness seeing It as All temporary ~
manifestation, conditioning, Identity, duality, lost in their head.
Told this name is who I Am; Me, Mine not going beyond Mind.
From FORMLESSNESS ~ making Divine life into an 'Object'.
Karma dragging the past into the future ~ Now is the future!
Wrong movement It's so simple * Mind wants it complicated.
It has to have a Mental Concept ~ Psyche*emotions for all!
Identifying with FUNCTION, the Content not the changing ~
The empty cup can be filled ~ Spirit transcending the body.
Once you accept its fulfillment, Life gives you everything.
'To Resist Is to Persist' ~ It won't last so don't fight it!
'There is No Good or Evil there's only Thinking about it.'
Totality giving you something to Understand, not to react.
A demonstration of Unconsciousness until Accepting this.
It's all Ego until blissful awareness of Unconditional Love.
If you know that and can Accept it there is Transcendence ~
It's not what's happening ~ I Am the SPACE for what happens.
Enjoy Consciously whatever's Formless, its Space Awareness.
Not judging you see the Life-Force accepting you are Natural ~
Losing the 'now' hang-ups; No Concepts, no I Am Eternal Truth.
Space of Consciousness is the Subject * its Content is the Object.
Our own Inner Stillness that we feel is being Aware of yourself.
Worry and suffering, his real pain, inventing more Illusions
leading us to Hell ~ Transmuting these negatives into bliss.
Truth is the Consciousness of Bliss ~ 'No Panic if Organic'
Evil Ego sitting on the Throne of Self-Identity, 'ME*KING'*Raja Tsar!
Kids throwing stones, outgunned by Drones, the Despot hasn't left!
Clearing the brain of Separation delusions! I'm me, they're them ~
Nature gives life ~ Conscious of every atom in the whole Universe.

Spiritual ~ Essence
* Infinite * Peace * Love * Rock & Roll * Conscious * Free* Space*
Falling in Illusion ~ Loved the last delusion, Formed in your brain.
Even for one of your delicious blowjobs I couldn't love you again ~
Reignite the spark that you betrayed & drowned in my pain & tears!
"You don't exist in her world anymore!" ~ Ringing loudly in my ears.
Sad & disappointed, Mental-World left with all these unreal meanings.

*

Planet * No Mind
Ask yourself a simple question,
who would you rather have as the next US. President,
Mrs.Clinton, Mr. Bush's dynasty or Edward Snowden & Why?
Cosmic Ocean* Eternal Universe*Conscious of Time ~ Meaning,
Mental-Form is created by your Mind in Omniscient Spacefulness
And I Love your Reflection of In/sanity, my perception Outside me.
'It is what it is' only if you understand your actions Consciously ~
or they're only words of selfish Ignorance not sharing in any bliss.

*

'They Gold Bars All Over the Place!'
Thinking's not all cracked up as it's meant to be ~
He's killing the Environment, animals, with our money!
Geography don't make you happy, oblivious to Wealth!
"In Tahiti they think they've died and gone to Heaven"
Hippy Pirates, stoned Love means your heart is working.
'Be here now' ~ keep reminding yourself of this mantra.
'The grass is always greener on the other side of Ego'
"If she phoned me up and said she'd met a hairy Cossack
sitting on top of her you'd also be delighted wouldn't you?"
She's a screamer famous for bad choices and consequences!
I was holding her hand ~ Innocence is bliss; Her crazy magicness.
'The ones who have empathy & the ones who don't have empathy'
Mescaline at sea, got off at Bora Bora's marae, good for your soul.

51

In the Mud is good

Let's have some 'Happy Therapy!' An explosive character.
'I like to hit the high desert in my lingerie and high heels'
"Selected by a sniper and shot Not for throwing stones!"
The most distance between people is misunderstanding!
Communicating from the heart ~ through Divine Space

*

New Conception

Persian Goddesses in a field of ecstatic golden Gazelle.
I had to let her go she gave herself up to another Satyr.
All illusionary feelings were razed in my emotional auras.
"If there's any hippies on the Pleiades please get in touch"
Wide, sultry eyes caressing my crystal mountain Obelisk.
All coming to the Temple of an immaculately shaved Pussy.
"Bring me my harem, bring me my blonde spiritual Angels!"
Breaking every Taboo to be free, nothing to hold onto ~
Just be who you are.

*

Mentalised Abstraction ~ 'Illusions R Us'

Life*energy Is Consciousness*Awareness of Itself*Stilling the Mind.
The Real eyes, 'How you gonna run from what's Inside Your brain?'
That's a good question, just sit down and observe it some would say;
It's just a theatre running in y/our head ~ All Mental-Formations/Ego!
Hooks our attention when we are really * Omniscient Self-Realisation
in Omnipresent Space & we're full of Unconditional love not a miasma!
Receiving Light* that says everything is alright in this Present moment
can't be grasped by Mind ~ No Mental Activity! We are it, Emptiness.
There's no Conspiracy as there's no 'them' all delusional programming.
The Acid comedown is great, more attractive than Cocaine dissociation!
Erasing all memory tapes ~ Zero Space of thought; Stillness in Silence.
Mind can't comprehend ~ Consciousness can't define it * as You Are It!
Only Identifying limitations of Life's energy ~ Reality is from No Thinking.

Translations of Presumption

Narcissistic personality disorder is a mental disorder in which people
have an inflated sense of their own importance, a deep need
for admiration and a lack of empathy, remorse for others.
But behind this mask of ultra confidence lies a fragile
self-esteem that's vulnerable to the slightest criticism.
"All animals are Equal but some are more Equal than others'
"You can demonstrate the way we want you to but not riot!"
'Innocent until proven guilty, Guilty until proven Innocent.'
It only takes one to really fuck you up! Keep looking, knocking,
eventually you'll find a door was always Open, ask your Muse.
Sufis whirling, Silent 'No Mind' ~ A Mindful*Conscious essence.
Blissful spinning Psychedelic girls surrounded by Mango trees.
All put to the sword! The Tipping Point of Un/Consciousness ~
Invisible weapons - letting them poison you to become Immune!
They hate the adults surely murdering all the women & children.
Genghis Khan's brain, a Massacre at the gates of Samarkand!
Mental-Formations ~ Where is the Innocence on Planet Earth?
Then they want to be the Master Race reinforcing their EGOS!
Done for a reaction, looking at my own response to see myself.
Not meant to be unhappy if I don't want to be ~ Surrendering.
Why can't people live together in Peace? Accepting what Is ~

*

Bamyan Emotional Trauma!

What is Holy? Insane Jihadists, demonic, barbaric, tragic ~
Fear is their Key, facing Murderous Genocide in their soul!
Why do they do it Nimrod? Don't know any f..... different!
Women are always raped & pillaged You can't make it up!
Separated with three red roses ~ from a Dervish angel.
Takes away your pain, withdrawal from the Addiction!
Divorced online ~ Meant to be at that time......
'We break our own hearts'

Insane ethnic hatred or Bom Shiva!
From around the corner ~ No one knows what's there!
The Biggest sex organ ~ the brain, in la maison de Plaisir.
You see what you wanna see, then they're fucked up for you.
Doing your Puja, double brandy and chocolate shake at sunset.
*WHITE LIGHT TANTRICS ~ Up up up * going out of the Mind-set.*
Krishna devotees singing, dancing, exhaling it all out. Psychedelic
getting a Kundalini rush from a chillum releasing a toast to Shiva!
In every heart with every breath
Nectar ~ essence of the Divine

*

Everyone's Whirligig
*Monkey Mind * How much is that Icelandic lettuce?*
Giant Super markets extorting people to the Max!
The system can only persecute, prosecute so much!
Everything is Love of the Divine not the Fear of God!
It's illegal to be a Sufi ~ In Ecstatic trance with Rumi.
Devotee in a frenzy, primeval feelings of fire inside.
*Behold everything is One * the holistic Energy ~*
Raw, elemental, unifying all beings & the Planet.
Kundalini take it in ~ feeling if it's working for you.
In states of Orgasmic bliss takes a line of MDMA.
Now You do your dream state. ~ Fun in the Sun

*

'You voted Tory You're a Cunt!
'We must warn you that some of our viewers
may find these images disturbing.' Bullshit!
Don't always look behind in your wing mirror
or you'll miss what's right in front of your eyes!
This deeper pain is just a heavy sensation to help
you realise life's illusion, to observe equanimously.
'Turn to the Sun and the shadow is behind you'

True Love Magnetism

Put a muzzle on it, it's barking between your legs!
If I'm a happy person I'll put about good energy.
Lamp of Love ~ Passion pussies burning brightly.
Then the tide comes in and takes it all away ~
Drowning in a whirlpool of unrequited Loving.
You need a Conjugal house for a pussy to purr.
A tribe of apes walkin' upright across the Savannah
*three million years ago * It's a long way down mate!*
Our minds have been programmed to be separated.
The Honeymoon State if you got food on the table.
Spread the Loving kindness as much as you can;
Most fertile. It's not a War it's Insane Genocide!
Need more Love in the World, beauty of dropping beyond.
*Going to the Source ~ Open Mind * Open Heart * Open Space.*

*

Mirroring It as Thyself

"Thou shalt Not commit Genocide!!" "Thou shalt realise all Life is a sacred gift
*to nurture * Thou shalt know why you are being f...ing wound up!" "Thereby*
Shalt thee know thy true ignorant, sociopathic enemy's reflection" "Thou Shalt
not give any pain or suffering even to little Grasshoppers" "Thou shalt become
Conscious ~

*

Targeting Your Market with a Drone!

*Dedicated to higher consciousness * Unconditional Love ~*
Men Totally respect y/our daughters, y/our mothers and wives.
Awareness of the bio*energy ~ Two souls fusing together inside.
Shrutti*Bhuti, Sacred ash, elemental super conductor ~ Heart
of all Charas' chakras; Alchemic Parties in a Samadhi Valley.
Auras consumed in the flames of super passionate Ecstasy.
'Reste calme et Profite de la vie ~
Really there is No one in Control!

'Socrates' Idealist'

The 'Corruption' is Bigger than any ideals of Democracy.
Paid that one back ~ I was left with the hard way out!
I did it to hold up the Higher Consciousness dream.
Walking the Walk of Unconditional Love with you ~
Different ways of Interpreting, Seeing, Living, Loving.
'I'm more Conceptual!' ~ Receiving it from where?
Peacock Angels on the roof of the dome of a Rock.
What's calling me? The Holy Grail of Rainbows.
More magical ladybirds and honey bees the better ~
Biting heads off preying Mantises before copulating!
So fertile the man pollinating! * Il Fungo Magico *

*

Vibrator's Experience * Pearls of Wisdom

'Live it, love it or get the fuck out of it!'
"I know You Goddess ~ I Am an Angel of Love"
Heaven is in Loving Your Pain ~ making you smile.
Loving sacred space with a full heart and spirit soul
There's Divine light all over her body * of Devotional poetry.
M A G I C A L*T A N T R I C A L*P S Y C H E D E L I C A L
About leaving the Mind booster behind ~ We need more Sufis!
Going down ley lines women spinning in the night making hay.
Walking in the wild Luberon after the Peach and Pear season.

*

Direct from Bliss to Non-Existence

"Why was it so Painful? Because it was so Real!"
"I didn't dump you for another man; I betrayed you for
another Lifestyle vision ~ With another man!" Absolutely
Her dreams didn't come true, lost in a mind full of dualities.
Consequences of going to the deepest levels of infatuation!
She held my hand then let me go without even a goodbye.
Lost the Trust ~ "WE ALL have Feelings too!" Om Shanti.

'Indian Democracy!'
Invasive Brain hacking software.
"We looked at that whole Modi Show, heard only an echo"
Going to the Taj Mahal with her for a coded message."
Show me your meteorite set in the opalescent marble ~
*Mysteries of our Alien genes * Collective precognition.*
I don't see it with Indian eyes. I'm only a 'foreigner'
How about Chinese or a Tibetan TakeAway?
People understand with their Open Heart.

*

Chitradurga's "Bom Bholenath!"
There's psychedelics & there's Love Psychedelics.
Taking Venus on a Golden Paradise honeymoon.
Going to the end of a Cosmic rainbow entwined
*Holding water lilies * identifying a bird of light.*
"I fell deep in Love with her in Hampi"
'Mothers give life they don't take it!'
Don't lose your 'Freedom Pass'
Brought up sitting on the lap
of a holistic chillum smoker!
Drinking Apollo Juice
A proper Bhang lassy,
& classic charas cake.

*

He have me away...
He Loves his Chemicals!
Buddha with light blue eyes ~
Genesis' early Universal particles....
Hunting for wobblers on a red Dwarf star.
Who's blowing the bubbles closer to a state of Nothingness?
'The Inspiration we seek is Inside us all ~ be quiet and listen.'

<u>At the Peaceful Heart Sutra Gate</u>
"No need to clap ~ Silence is the biggest gift"
It's horrible to be caged especially if you're a parrot chained to a stick.
'Can't have blockages the more Open you are the more Free you are'.
What are your aspirations more than money? All to be Free & Happy
"Let me come inside your Mind and feel your Omnipresence ~"

*

<u>Can't make her</u>
The woman can't change your life
She can fulfill your Life; Makes it more complete
To be Ultimately your happiness ~
How Intimately do you want to go?
Is it Multi-Delusional in the Multi-Dimensional?
Living in an impenetrable forest of sacred plants.
All wrecked together ~ lots of heavy purring.

*

<u>Who's Crazy Now?</u>
Slagging off the Whistleblowers with more distractions!
'No comment', letting people make up their own Minds.
You can't have it because you're a smart Eunuch Robotic.
Kept secret, why is it denied? Running out of Untouchables!
"I'll believe it when I see it with my own eyes
but I won't disbelieve it if I haven't seen it"
I intuited it in the feelings vibrating in a crystal ball.
Now excess of Labour Units, Human Capital widgets.
Poisoning the rivers ~ bringing the population down!
Shoot first ask questions later, train that Slave pack!
Changed from a human being to beating the fuck out
of their own people; They will never understand it!
Criminalising the whole country, you got a record;
You're a f....g baddie ask any Aborigine!

In My Space
Respect all this Freedom ~
You're coming into my Aura fields!
The Truth is always there in essence.
But the lies are more visible ~ don't go
in my trip and run ~ We're under Attack!

*

'Semites with a Twist!'
Mind's-eye illusion* observing something beyond Magical.
Boddhisattvas who think too much; Be Silent Atomic Stillness.
He's just living Now * sitting in smiling Awareness ~ of Form.
In Space we manifest an Object, the fractal brain is its receiver
Symbiosis * harmonising with nature, trees giving us Oxygen;
Giving life to humans and us being its Consciousness of Life.
Swooning brunette butterflies sizzling in the fire.

*

Plants Making Music*Jasmine's glistening white petals.
What's the sound of the sacred Tulsi, sweetest melodies of
Frangipani, exquisite Rose telepathy from a Sufi poet, Rumi;
1000 petalled lotuses in full bloom and the rhythms of Champa
arrows fired from Kamadeva's bow ~ Being dipped in Euphoria.

*

'Southern Electric' * Industrialised Monkeys
He's recharging not recovering for the next until it's finished.
'God knows what it means!' ~ "Don't blame me I'm bipolar!"
'We are currently experiencing a high call volume
and our queue times are longer than usual.'
So employ more people give a better service!
That would go against Your highest profit motive.
All 3 Fukushima nuclear reactor cores have 100% melted!
Nicest thing anyone's said to me today, 'treasure yourself'.
'Life on a mole of dust suspended on a sunbeam' C. Sagan.

<u>Yet the Earth will feed us</u>
The famous Martian silken worm coated in Golden thread.
When you gotta fight your brother for a piece of bread!
'It's really hard on the poor'; Did you put a lock on it?
There's no money in making a 60 year old light bulb!
Unstable Nuclear plantations it's all about profits!
Something there before the Big Bang...
See how blind addiction makes us all?
'Piercing the Corporations' dark veil.'
Pre*existing is Nothing to know ~
No time or space ~ Why Kill it?

*

<u>Poverty Cameo</u>
A man with no money
A man with no cow
A man with no wife
A man with no family
A man with not a lot
"Welcome*Enchanter"
Kwan Yin with no sin
Living close to nature ~
Drinking from a still, pure pool.
Reflections of a clear blue sky.
The Chief has a young wife ~
In those looks of their eyes.
Let Life Be.

*

<u>'Incredible India'</u>
"When you come around you won't know how much blood is flowing!"
Got smashed up lost my trust and nerves ~ bent my pinky!
"I just think you gotta become One
with the garbage"

Is it the right definition?
"I don't smoke 'em but I like to roll 'em"
Releasing the Fear ~ just a little bit higher dear!
Locked into business cycles or a heart full of generosity?
Let me come inside your Mind and feel your Omnipresence.
I'm willing to play the game and dance with you Magically.
Realising the listening Is your Awareness ~ not the words
but the Energy in the words ~ feeling a musical Love melody.
Fulfill the purpose of {y/our} Life "If you resist things will persist."
Bom Bholenath, Bom Shiva; Recording a history of the Illusionary!
It's that we still believe in it, that it exists. Be synergy * Spontaneous
You wanna be on the good side of God, who isn't in Love with you?
Coming back expanding Universe ~ dissolving in the transmutation.
Sharing this sub-atomic feeling with the whole of life.
'Divine is the light inside all of us' * In Cosmic Space.

*

Oxytocin Box of Chocolates
The Spontaneous Spirit is with you ~
"DM Tryptamine we have quite a lot in our brain"
This stuff is not in the Pill it's in the brain chemistry!
Triggering more Space to get synergy naturally high ~
Getting the right signals from the carriers ~ More Serotonin!
'The falling in Love chemical' ~ with endo-cannabinoid bliss.
Try some psyche*active Hemp oil, Cannabis opening receptors!
Feeding the brain the right Adrenalin ~ keep getting the Ecstasy!
Very expansionist on Acid! Heat changing the molecules of her bud.
"In the hole we all work together it's a whole different effect!"
Super drugs ~ We can choose what we Love to experience.
Making me very high in my Pan synergetic dreams.

When do you Understand

"The Richest people are all Archon Satanists" he said.
Half the World's population lives in a hole in the road!
Just remember all the good times sumptuous Aphrodite.
You wouldn't give it up living in your Palace would you?
Not gonna lose the Power of his golden throne is he?
Global mayhem in order to keep their Empires going.
The top of the hill is Utopia no mistaking that!
We had the Vision of a lifetime.
There's a lot of Magic there.

*

Power for the Party

Forms in the Formless Ocean.
'The Obstacle lighting your way ~
Consciousness ~ what we embrace.
Fly Atlantis "We're all getting Smarter."
"There's a lot of High functioning addicts!"
Whether Good or bad karma who are we to
make judgments ~ Illusions of Y/our MIND?
Loving the dream ~ bringing each other up.

*

Scratch, Sniff & Snitch!

Slightly wrong here; Grassing on yur neighbor!
"I thought it was Love yur neighbor as Yourself"
Not hate yu neighbor, greedy, jealous judgments.
"Relax Baba, what can you do about it?" Witnessing.
But it's knowing there's nothing you can do about it ~
And be Consciously chilled, manifesting our soap operas.
Conditioned drive moaning about what other people are doing.
Sign up ~ You get a digital Character and a virtual Spaceship.
I have one piece of Software ~ Synchronised to Internally Divine.

Undercurrent of Life Stream

'In Buddhist psychology the process of the changing mind is manifested in two levels or streams. The subconscious stream 'Bhavanga Citta' and the Conscious stream 'Vithi citta'. Each one merges into the other. The subconscious stream is the hidden repository of all the impressions and memories of thoughts that pass through the conscious mind. All experiences and tendencies are stored up there, but they exert an influence over the conscious mind without it being aware of the source of this influence. These two streams of mind being conditioned by each other. The state of the active conscious mind and awareness is generally present during the day when one is awake. It is conscious of all impacts and impressions continually received from outside, through the 5 senses or of sensations received from within by way of ideas or thoughts or recollections of former thoughts. When this conscious stream which is constantly receiving sensations from within or without subsides into inactivity, as for instance during sleep, the other stream the subconscious (Bhavanga Citta) manifests ~ flowing like an undisturbed stream so long as the conscious stream does not arise to disturb it through the sense channels. When awake every time an arisen thought of the conscious mind subsides and before the next thought can arise within that infinitesimally minute fraction of time, the subconscious stream intervenes. Then when the next thought of the conscious mind level arises the subconscious stream subsides into inactivity. Since innumerable thoughts arise and fall one after another during the day so then there are innumerable momentary interruptions to the flow of the subconscious stream during the day. The subconscious is referred to as a state of subliminal activity, viz. an activity that takes place below the threshold of the conscious mind, an activity of which therefore there is no awareness on the conscious mind. The conscious stream holds only one thought or idea at a time whereas the subconscious stream holds all the impressions of all the thoughts, ideas and experiences that enter and leave the conscious mind. This subconscious life stream allows us to have a memory, conditioning our thinking and action. The Bhavanga is the 'bhava' (existence) & 'anga' (factor) 'Bhavanga Citta' is the indispensable factor or basis of existence.

The factor of life by means of which the flow of existence or being is maintained without a break the continuing basis or undercurrent of life, the stream of existence keeping life going. This stream of being is an indispensable condition of individual life. It is comparable to the current of a river when it flows calmly on, unhindered by any obstacle and when that current is opposed by any thought from the world within or perturbed by tributary streams of the senses from the world without then thoughts in the conscious mind stream arise. There is a juxtaposition of momentary states of consciousness subliminal and suprasubliminal throughout a lifetime'

*

From 'Rebirth Explained' by V. Gunaratna.
Buddhist Publication Society (BPS). Kandy, Sri Lanka.1980
This essential conscious ~ subconscious life stream is felt as a flow of sensations on the body/mind; An equanimous, detached awareness of this ever changing flow of sensations, 'Sampaggana Satimo' is 'Vipassana, Insight Meditation' (As taught by S N Goenkaji & U Ba Khin, www.dhamma.org). Used in practice to help us realise our true Inner Cosmic being. See BPS; 'The Four Sublime States' by Nyanaponika Maha Thera.

*

It's an Ocean within You
*"Searching for God is like a fish searching for water" Going into seclusion, hibernation, contemplation, immersion. An Artist Is Consciousness of the Paradox of Time * Space Love is who we are ~ all radiating, tuning in our Telepathy 'Planet Psychedelia' Book of Spells of Human experiences! Quantity or EQuality! 'Are You a Mind-Controlled Slave?' Fire the arrow > Feeling the beating heart of the others. Being free thought ~ Love Is Empathy*

Why Not?

I don't wanna know the future, it's a Mystery.
Not gonna find Nirvana at a Psychic Fair ~
Goddesses telling yur Mrs. to 'fuck off!'
Accepting things as they are,
fatally doomed from the Start!
"You Create your own flow ~
Doing exactly what I wanna do,
doing what comes high naturally."
Straight from the heart of 'Incredible India'
'They think the country's Spiritual not the people!'
Who the fuck knows anything really?

*

Fertility Charms of a Sufi Superwoman*

The Biggest fright of her life ~ resonating lifelong trauma, passing it on!
See what it's like right on the Edge! Her life is bigger than the weather.
Moment between life & death ~ constantly being present.
'Nudism is Prohibited Punishable under section 249'.
He believes it, he's witnessed it; Step1, be here now.
Heaven is Hell and every kind of Temptation inside!
Not schizophrenic where you go out of existence ~
'Picasso was the greatest painter.' Really so what?
Narcosis coming up too fast ~ raptures of the deep!
Bi*Polar snorkeling*Psychedelic, hallucinogenic reefs.
Fixated on one cowrie, her gorgeous undulating Yoni.
Ecstatic * States * Most * light is at the Top.

*

Rumi

"The core of the feminine comes directly as a ray of the Sun
Not the earthly figure you hear about in love songs;
There's more to her mystery than that. You may say she's
not from the manifest world at all ~ but the creator of it."

<u>Green Rainbow Radar.</u>
A Monk's Diamond Throne.
The Mudras of Buddha
Vishnu ~ Universal God.
"She's Sitting on a Big Naga!"
Tree of Life with sweet Jasmine
You Have The Goddess in You.

*

<u>A Plate of Smoke</u>
That's the Trick! There's gotta be enough DMT in the System
to knock out the Self! More Psychedelic trance at Shiva Valley.
Rebalancing 'Growth' will need to STOP at the Red light!
Where the Chillum smokers live, get best hash, Espresso.
Sacraments at the Sante Daime Church, over the Pulpit!
Better to grow your own Original Jamaican if you can.
Exotic medicine scraped off the back of a Kambo toad!
Maintaining the crazy illusion of the War On Drugs.
Just chill out and put a Star by that one!

*

<u>Intra Space <*> Space</u>
All this Love that I know that I Am.
'For sure I'd be a Mutineer on the Bountiful in Noa Noa'
GB. ~ They've Sold the model to fuck all the people up!
"Go start a Revolution ~ need to Reboot the System!"
Putting your head through a Portal of Loving Kindness.
The Real medicine is in its Awareness.
Can't always be at the Copacabana ~
That you're Knowing it all changes.
The Ultimate mantra is 'Fuk It!'
The Numbers are out and ..?
This Love is Unconditional

Earth * United

Slave wages in the Amazon ~ Zero hour contracts.
Automated, centralized control, flying Smart drones.
Freeing up humanity; Send it to a f….. 3D Printer!
Becoming Sentient * never turn the soil, no separation.
Going back to Hemp ~ In a High altitude Cannabis field.
Oxygenator, homeopathic cure, a Harmonically tuned Planet.
Pulsing, fertile Oasis in the middle of nowhere. Global diversity.
Recycling Sunshine, full Moon eclipse over the Himalayas ~
"Came down from Muktinath on a beautifully fresh Spring day."
Nature left by itself ~ creating all this Stuff, fruit of the desert.
Rebuilding Organic harvest meadows, keeping it moving.
"Pachamama will do whatever Pachamama does"
We're the 99.00% saving their Gold Ass! Why?
There's no way we're taking Control of Nature!
4 or 5 plants living in a tent in your bedroom.
We can't see it for what it truly is.
Mountains full of breathing moss.
Confusing all the Predators

*

"I never want to ride a bike up a hill!"

"I don't Know because there's nothing to Know!"
Who is this 'I' who doesn't want to know, asking the question?
It's all the Divine and being in full devotion to it.
This Life needs the illumination of the Sun * Consciousness'
Believing in 'Me' - Freedom to be ~ after I left the monastery.
Knowing your own Sat*guru. Opening Your Soul Baba.
Hippies in Wonderland, a trick to your enlightenment.
Keeping your brain busy with 'Spiritual Mythology'.
I can't talk to them, they found God; I found Joy.
Poesie in the bursting grains of the Sun.

"I've been on Hawaii"
Liquid Sunshine Summer
Invisible nature ~ 'A reality of duality'
However you're dreaming of beyond ~
Age of Aquarius having a Heart Attack!
A willing Slave who is devoted to loving me!
Possessed by an Evil, selfish dark bad Spirit
Possessed by their own Ego entity Identity.
Not Surrealism but Paranoia, Fears & Desire.
Needing another Ideal frequency to Re/Activate me.
Human Beings, not Caste ~ No more Separateness.
No reactions of Shopkeeper & Customer only Bhakti.
Meeting all Life ~ FORMS reacting to the primary role.
Because they hate the Adults they'll kill their children!
"I Love my Narcissism" ~ Sensations of Divine delusion.
*"Seek ye first the inner * dimensional Paradise*
all the things you thought you really wanted
will eventually be made known unto you."
Then in Heavenly Consciousness.
The Space of Life.

*

Serious in Hell
Trapped in an Economic nightmare that we
can never comprehend! So what do you do?
Just your selfish Ego soaking in an Eco hole!
'Good things happen to Good people ~'
"They can survive on virtually Fuck All!"
*'Where did the Psy*trance scene go?'*
Life is Enlightened by itself.
"I Am Not a Prisoner!"
Being Self - Induced

To Resist It

Splinters in your field of whole consciousness ~
A Vast Space & we reduced it to just an Object!
This Experience is pure perception in the Mind.
I licked Khmer Kali she was a velveteen dream!
Conceptual creation*figments of my imagination.
'We're all Angels here!'

*

Ego Devils - becoming separate!

Wavelengths ~ living & dying in each moment of Life.
You dropped your Love for me like a radioactive stone
in the swollen river and your soul screamed, 'fuck off!"
"Can't see me in a relationship if I can't be myself"
Universality ~ People don't get it!
Identity of the Self ~ Mind-Object.
Forgot her she killed my brother!
A Mind-Form, "She Loves Me!"
She becomes Me/Mine/Myself.
As just a temporary expression ~
of the whole ~ "I want this, Possession!"
Completely lost the love of any togetherness.
Subconscious to Subconscious * Souls' love.

*

Mr. Fuck in Sinville

"I get laid more without a girlfriend than with one!"
"How do you expect a Goldfish to climb a tree?"
"Try everything you'd be surprised at what you like"
Truth is the truth no need to remember, unlike a lie.
You can worship whatever you like at the Temple of Love.
God is outside Time ~ S/he wasn't created until Mythology.
Kamadeva sent by God to plough her fields.
Addicted to the dreaming ~ Back to Reality!

Than what it was!
Throwing petrol on the fire exploding into a bigger inferno!
Drop her like a hot rock! Sulk, sulk, sulk, sulk, snap, gone!
"I left you in so much pain!" Downloading your comedown!
Shut the f... up you're not ruining my day; Don't feed, feel it.
No respect, no honesty, no mercy, too negative for my liking!
No understanding ~ Seeing a Smile as a sign of weakness.
"You control your body with your Mind not your eyes ~"
It's not what you do it's how you do it ~ Good feelings!
"Buddha sent them to me so I took them"
'Brother from another mother'

*

Multi*Dimensional*Trance*Freedom
"I got the Energetic weapon gun*you got Elementals!"
White light energy the Great Spirit flowing underneath.
Coming from Nature ~ Mind-tripping Karma mania.
Undominated - "Progress ain't always pretty!"
Baby Speed! Putting a name to a conception,
good karma, bad karma, Cosmic non-karma.
"Build us a Bigger Bomb!" "Get off my screen!"

*

This is how I feel now ~ 'As we are'
"Did you ever see an Elephant egg?"
"Tu ne peux pas regarder les poissons!"
Conditional Pain * Unconditional Love
And Wonders * at the Ecstatic Bliss of Mars & Venus*
Those honeybees, sweet Cherubim * in playful harmony.
Change means it comes ~ goes somehow ~ comes again.
I am not so pure but my heart beats * with desire divine.
Facing into the Sun the Golden alchemy*existing as true.
Making me & you

<u>Goenkaji</u>
'Can kundalini be awakened by the practice of Vipassana?
What is kundalini? Kundalini is the activation of nerve centres on
the spinal cord. By the practice of Vipassana, every atom of the
body gets activated. Kundalini is just a small part of that. Practice
Vipassana you'll easily understand the difference between the two.
*

<u>King Cobra ~ Long & Very Fast!</u>
'Heard it's not a good idea to still be a virgin in Paradise!'
'You want to be FREE ~ to do what makes You HAPPY'
"Sex is a physical act and Love is an emotional choice!"
We come with a great hope & end up sad; Now prefer Renters!
"When you're married they're in Control & you're super fucked
by a 16 year Princess of poverty!" Accepting it and letting it go.
If the penis don't work she's out the contract onto another job.
People growing apart it's how things are ~ Dial a Wet Uterus!
When pussy's in your face everyday, OK I had enough purring.
They're not happy with themselves, looks down on other people.
You find Buddha ~ Buddha finds You, don't force it on anyone!
Humans we're All Cosmic ~ Whose God created the Heaven?
"Khmer comes to a village marries a girl takes her to Thailand;
Then having a baby with her brother, sells her to a Whorehouse!"
Giggling & having a laugh ~ they got feeling; 'Sawadee Krap!'
Meaning who wants to take Responsibility?
*

<u>Kama* Rati* Honey*Moon</u>
It's so difficult to let go when you are a Light worker with her Love hooks!
Instantaneous * Consciousness, Infinite Space for Unconditional Love ~
Shiva Shakti*don't like the word 'Illusion' change it for 'dreaming stream'
I'm happy to have some Free, Still Space ~ to send Love beams to you.
Need a higher 'Ideal of Love' to pull you out of Romantic love's delusion!

71

Blue eyed Tigers & Velvety Smooth Pussies

"I want Now ~ no doors in-between!"
They can create you a yarn. She has Power!
An Apsara turning up with her own bag of icicles.
'If you're nice to me I'm nice to you' Simple.
Some very beautiful women riding bicycles.
The realisation of the true feelings of LOVE ~
I am deep, we were deep, not an easy extraction!
To walk away and leave Venus' Temple behind.
As I ride off into the sunset * Big Bang #4!

*

Purring Planet ~ Consciously

Have your wet orgasms come to an end yet?
You take away my hand and you turn your back
from my caresses & fall asleep, what's left now?
In the back of a Limousine with a bevy of hot Divas!
Didn't have Demons in my head until she'd parked,
another man in our love bed! Betrayed all the Trust.
Jealous? "It is what it is until it's something else!"
What was this great lesson you came to learn?
'You do what makes it right and be happy'
Drops in the Heart ~ All About that Time!

*

It Collapses

As plane as the light of day on your face.
An unbelievable Shift in Consciousness ~
"You go through a certain amount of SUFFERING
And You Surrender!" ~ The change is in Myself.
"looks like we have Nothing more to say" 'WOW!'
Feeling that Pain through ACCEPTANCE
The Here Now ~ this Is what Is * Absolutely!
Underneath ~ LIFE Is Still * Present.

72

<u>Eid (dedicated to Alan Henning another Innocent person murdered!)</u>
I never understood it when I heard that there are those that willfully
profit from Wars. Yet we Never hear about these vested interests in
the mainstream media! It's another one of those 'follow the money'
paradigms! All these warring lunatics seem to be Armed to the teeth
by whom and why, what is the supplier's motivation apart from more
economic Power? There's those counting their $£% profits in the
devastation, stirring it up, supplying everybody who wants Battle
Axes! Unbelievably to most 'humans' they want War Not Mercy!
Don't expect any for these are human sacrifices to their Gods
of Crimes Against Humanity! Cosmic Inshallah Is Empathy!

*

<u>An Angel with his Severed Head!</u>
Is this what they like to call 'Collateral Damage' then!?
No cries of forgiveness, mercy or peace on this eve of Eid!
Obsessional Jihadis running the mosque next to the Arsenal!
"Of course we're fighting a War of Invasive Occupation mate!"
Not a propaganda name game of who is most barbaric!
When your whole village was Obliterated by a Drone
from Texas and your family Blown to smithereens
at a wedding by Tomahawk missiles from a clone!
What would your surviving son do brother?
A revengeful Soul laid to rest in Paradise!

*

<u>Suicidal Love Chimera</u>
You don't want Love ~ your ego sent me home alone again!
You want Love with a list of demands, needs & securities!
Love is Not enough for you but it's your big delusion.
Just so we're clear on this uber bargain of Emotions;
This is not deep conscious sensitivity at all ~ faking it!
You killed your feelings & me at the deepest Level.
Sign on the door, 'Please do not disturb in Samadhi'

Ultra Sensitivity

Bathing together in the Lotus Heart's pool ~ purely physical.
"Don't have to go looking for grief ~ Grief will soon find you"
Muktalingham melting deep in a Yoni crucible of devotion.
Someone you can never let go of ~ It's terrible!
"How do you deal with that much Love!"
Smiling on the lips of her Universe.
Strong powerful, grinding hips.
Meditating on Eve breathing
In the Eco not Ego garden.

*

Fantastic Not Fanatic

Khmers behind every shaved bush, "Tuk tuk?" "Boom Boom?"
Freedom to lose my appetite for any Attachment to Spicy frog.
Feeling the Cosmic chorten spinning ~ cool energy at dusk.
Purple rays streaming, took her shoes off at Bayon's Temple.
Sacred designs of a million stones, Cambodian Rubik cubists.
When the Moon at night hits the light of a rare precious diamond.
Lost in an Astro-turf jungle, you'll need permission from the King!
A demon took away his wife and pounded her without permission!
If Guilty she couldn't look you in the face or even say another word;
Knew what she was doing, wasn't a thing about you only about herself!
She turned her back without a thought ~ left me to slowly drown alone!
Love is to honour ~ serve and surrender to each other forever more.

*

Disengaged

"If you don't do what we say - We BOMB YOU!"
It's that simple! Who wants to step on a Baby Cobra?
You don't want to be stung by a big Scorpion ant either.
'The beauty doesn't last long but the poison gets stronger'
Salary paid as beer tokens; "I was FREE I could Leave."
I wanted her to be as a beautiful, swooning Mariposa

What's in the Seed Bank?

"Wake up don't you want to create ~ be something truly amazing?"
Slaughter Beach, 70,000 dead fish washed ashore ~ no more!
A Bluish whale brought us a message within its stomach full of
plastic trash. 30,000 bees destroyed buzzing over GMO crops.
Towns living alongside a toxic chemical site, they're f... Fracked!
Poisoning their rivers ~ Killing the people with more Chemtrails.
Destroying the Planet, no natural greens, Pachamama Genocide.
What you gonna eat from Mr. Monsanto?
Diabolical, Now it makes complete sense;
They're making all the wrong decisions
On purpose!

*

Sociopathic Matrix

Psychologists in Control with Prof. Donald Fuck.
'Found a new passport lying in the Thermite dust!'
TV such a powerful tool making imprints in my head.
Brainwashed by her big tits, they're put there for you
to look at ~ pressing all the right buttons, squeezing buttocks.
Tune in after our corporate sponsor invades your empty space.
Repeat, repeat Programming, News Flash gets you in seconds.
Accessing All Areas feeding your brain telling you how it will be!
Critical thinker kept within the parameters of his favorite series.
"Excuse me where is the Sleeping Buddha?"
'I've finally healed my heart!'

*

Big Lips Reader

Legal & Tender ~ How far can you bend her
Into Shape ~ of her Goddess?
Living inside existing in her heart.
Create your Heaven

Learning Y/our Biggest Lesson

What is it? A Blessing and a curse.... (in a hidden disguise)
The human condition*duality ~ Illusion * Revelation, knowing it!
Reflections of y/our behaviour to uphold this changing reality ~
Feeling is the constant of these ~ Conscious of truthful harmony.
Allowing ourselves to experience the deepest human emotions
with someone we love, is rare ~ a sacred promise in y/our eyes.
Taking each other to beyond the limits of our hearts ~ in ONE
in trust, honesty, respect, ecstasy,
not in fear, anger, denial, rejection.
Being Aware of all these conditions
holding each other together sacredly
in Sweet bliss and in the raging storm
for myself and for the Divinely ~ Beloved.
They can so easily be broken ~ gone Forever to Infinity.
It is as it is, letting it go ~ is Realisation in Consciousness
not reaction losing all senses of the consequences of life.
Our Spirits can be broken in this choice of vulnerability.
Conscious of this delicate Sensitivity
Conscious of Mind ~ You and me.
Conscious of our actions, don't poison the flow.
Causes & effects at this pure magical depth!
Transcending our expectations ~ to be free.
I saw the Goddess in You ** Thank You.

*

'Che Sera Sera'

My mother used to sing that when she was young ~
The heart is the window to the Higher Consciousness.
Breathing Love Inhale ~ exhale, pranayama again!
"We All come from the same mother"
Sweet mango season in Mandrem.
Coming from a fast beating heart.

Viral
'Be Happy
*

Are they H A P P Y?
Do they Smile Baba?
Pirates who lost their way.
One of the Goa vibe experiences ~ Lost in Space.
No more FEELING left at the Psy*trance party vibe.
Selling a collection of mini linghams next to the Monopoly!
*

Where's My Devotee!
Favorite Program, 'Mind Infection' ~ 'It's All a Big Distraction!'
'Love is the most beautiful enchantment ~ in Time & Space'
Going deeper & deeper coming closer & closer to the honey,
*to losing our delusions * to understanding Space's illusions.*
Look in the eye of the other and have a good time.
Drop your Judgments for the senses to be alive!
"Without your brain you're a cabbage"
Do you think you're in the 5th dimension here Baba?
Inside Goa there's a lot to see and dream!
Freedom diving without a crash helmet!
*

'Crystalline Trace Formations'
Paradise Beach, in a hut with no walls.
"I always love the first smoke of the day"
"I was a hippy my boyfriend was a Skinhead"
Busted in Kathmandu! He's hiding under the table.
Angry Inside stress ~ We're All channels of Light
Shining on your DNA; Reflecting a Hologram of us.
Living It ~ Chasing Dreams, coming into a Love Temple.
Sun Worshipper on her knees!

<u>People's Believing</u>
'This is information that the people of the World should have' mate.
Whistleblowing 'The King is not a Buddha he can't do everything!'
Pressing both hands together ~ a moment of complete surrender.
Whatever the cost! Why be a devil with me? Realizing deceptions!
I bathed in lights of a moonlit night with Frangipani scented spirits.
Kissed Kali's jet black petals, sucked deep into her red velvet clam.
A super hot Apsara, Priya's sister licking my throbbing Muktalinga!
Being Conscious of our own feelings ~ vibrations happening.
We can feel the beating, sensitive heart of the other.
Not losing it, Peaceful Power ~ We Love
*

<u>Intimidation It's Evolution Even</u> ~
They're all seemingly fuckin' mad!
It's her Temple, sharing the meat ~
Kissing a holy jet meteorite vagina.
"Do what your mother wants Inshallah!"
Cultural Engineering ~ You can't flog
people for 200 years and come out clean!
Now is all that is and being Happy in it.
Only Existing in the Present moment ~
"Carefully thinking the next moment is
more important than the moment Now!"
Or you're just operating in the past delusions.
We only concept eulogize the Stars not the Space.
*** Not seeing the Consciousness ***
*

<u>Kahlil Gibran</u>
"There is something greater and purer than what the mouth utters.
Silence illuminates our souls, whispers to our hearts ~
and brings them together." ~ from 'The Broken Wings'

Then I'm Happy

"As long as I've got beans to make raw chocolate!"
Loving you is the greatest illusion in the Universe.
Revving Goa Enfields ~ "I tell my bike I love it every day!"
The Goddess' energy * "It's all about Emotions in Space"
Clones don't have souls, limits the sacrifices we can do!
Dying ~ "Just leave me in a room full of weed"
Embodying your natural divinity

*

Innocence is No excuse!

"If you don't grow a beard we'll chop your bollocks!"
Where's the News of the World when you want it?
"Unfortunately we're going to be the new Nazis!"
More trouble on the borders ~
Less lines of demarcation, less friction.
What the fuck do we know?
Nature itself is the complete balance.
'All the funky women hang out between the piers in Brighton'
Nature doesn't care what the colour of your car is!
It is all irrelevant

*

You can't make it up Baba!

I eat dead meat ~ My food eats salad.
"I'm not a Yogi, I'm not giving up passion"
I'm only Really a Hologram in carnal heat!
"It's Mind ~ No Heart or Soul… for some.
Otherwise they would have planted trees"
Disillusionment ~ I've given up on it all.
Crystals on the tip of the tongue.
All Tantra*d up!

'Only Temporary'

What makes one massacre more important News than another?
In that Stillness is the Wisdom ~ The 'You/r' Consciousness
realizing that it's Not Separate from the flowering * Life force.
She's a blushing Fanwallah, we'll come up with our own Eden!
Filtering the impurities, pathogens, coliforms forced outside ~
Bringing it back to life ~ how about seeing the bigger picture?
The Eternal manifesting into Infinite Forms in Multiversal Space.
Underneath that is one Cosmic Quantum, Soul train Mother!
On a Crystal mission, "Devil get behind me!"
Immature beavers can be really dangerous…

*

Ego Identity V Eternity

Win a Trip to Goa! ~ "LSD is a starting point"
Everything is alive through your own sensation.
Life Is timeless ~ The Point*NOW* IS FEELING IT.
Everything that Is ~ Is meant to be * It Is (reality).
A perfect time for the Love apple to fall off the tree!
How do I get what I want to get ~ Bio*Chemistry?
Mind-Objects are the Reflection within the Subject.
Dying is losing the 'Object.'
'LIFE'S * ENERGY * DOESN'T DIE'
Experiencing deep in you that which is INFINITE
Singularity ~ no duality * Polarity & delusionality.
Just that, the realization that YOU ARE
And it's Not another Object in Space!

*

Woman the Heart of the Divine

Don't need to sell our Kingdom, our Soul sister for it!
It's what the Devil plays; Have to be Authentic…..
Remembering the Conscious source ~
In the source, with the source feeling.

'My Mind!'

Every little touch making them cry out in anticipation!
Feeding your kids or buying a black current condom!
"Life is more than Ecocomics; For the best of one & All!"
In My Head, Identification ~ It's Me owning My chair & hair.
Self pity ~ You sent me spinning into a dark chasm darling!
Temporary things ~ All Mental-Form entities, learn to let go

*

Nothingness ~ Spiritual

Out of Your Mind ~ Observing not Obsessing!
Chi, Clarity, Life, Energy, Space, Infinitely ~
You can't make an Object out of the Form*less.
Can't attach anything to it but you can be Spirit.
All that Stuff…. Young lungs lighting the chillums!
A Civil War or beautiful girls with garlands in their hair.
You haven't lost it just changing to new, high vibrations ~
Something that makes the dream possible * Alive that Is!
The Conscious flow ~ that we naturally embrace, letting go.
Letting it BE

*

LOVE IS ALL

Free will ~ Feeling that you are/will be Always in Love.
Transmutation of these False beliefs of 'who you/we are.'
Fifty whiplashes of 1000 every Friday morning after prayers!
What sort of demonic tyranny are we accepting from despots?
Allowing yourself to be liberated in light plasma making contact.
And Not worshipping at the Temples of the God*desses of Ego.
Aware of all y/our Addictions, we give each other the freedom ~
Like being a butterfly fluttering its wings in a summer meadow.
'The hotter she is the more space in-between her molecules'
God gave you a beautiful mind & body so why suppress them?
Ecstatic magnetic pulsation Grenade at the Venus' Gate!

<u>Alert to the Present!</u>
Flying into the heart of the Sun.
Feeling Inside ~ what I AM IS
Listening with no thought ~
Existence Is Consciousness
The Infinite Subject appearing as an Object!
Who Am I? Not giving yourself an answer.
It's in the Stillness
*

*<u>All as One * One as All * Vibrations</u>*
On a different channel ~ receiving Milky-way Hi frequencies.
Allow it to unfold, to bloom into a galaxy of Sacred geometry.
*Connecting all the dots of nature * the flower of life is just there*
reflecting unimaginably ~ Divine in a pure way one more time!
You go through Hell to be Free ~ It's in each moment we live & die.
Allowance going through this fire and letting go in the experience.
Violet flame transmutator ~ transmitting through the darkness.
*The behavior to Love yourself more * Alight in the Nothingness.*
Fear coming in "No happy end to Love" "Is there ever an End?"
Let go ~ not to be in conflict fighting with/in y/ourselves.
Met her on the overnight bus to Bhaktipur looking for true ~
Happiness of unconditional loving bringing you inner peace.
*

*<u>Being Love Itself ~ Ever*Changing</u>*
*Sip and smell it * Love is an Illusion ~ It can & does disappear!*
It won't disappear because the Love is in essence inside each one of us.
"Life is like riding a bicycle to keep your balance you must keep moving ~"
Living in a gorgeous abandoned Palace with an Angel devotee of the light.
'Everything is energy ~ match a frequency to the reality that you want'
*"Be sure to wear some flowers in your hair * some gentle people there"*

<u>5HTP * Shell</u>
"I can hear the Ocean ~ Inside."
Cashadelic ~ 'Cash is a Global King'
"You can always start at 10 and go up,
you can't start at 20 and come down!"
'In the Safe is last place you hide treasure!'
*

<u>Everyone Is Love</u>
The gaps start appearing more in the Mind-stream ~
So You have less thinking being more open to our essential Space.
Subconscious pain body * emotions of humanity taking us for a ride!
Live experiments on living people! Still doing what my heart tells me
not what you say is right or wrong ~ you're only talking to an echo...
'Gives me the Waheebeejeebis, Barbaric, inhuman, demonic!'
"The only good one in it is the brave blogger getting flogged!"
Everyone wants Love ~ Everyone needs Love
When you Feel Yourself connected to All
*

<u>Lived with Fears for Years</u>
Be True to Yourself ~ Courage not lying to Yourself level.
Having to let go of all the 'naïve' Illusions you gave Yourself.
Taking away the Concentration of the people to something else
so you don't find yourself ~ remembering who you truly are!
"I saw the black hole and it was unnerving ** Very Cosmic"
And he said "if she really loved me she'd buy me drugs."
Taking drugs to escape! Escape what? Such amazing Reality.
One side of the wall was grey - black & white, not any colours.
The other side was full of Abstractions, Psychedelic patterns!
'They haven't invented that yet Baba ~ Spontaneous Intimacy.'
"There's more to this experience than whatever it seems to be"

<u>Very Subtle Channels</u>
Accepting the totality of Life ~
Brought about by Itself ~ 'Dhamma'
Our Ego comes in and judges it as Real.
Shaping me from a limited perspective ~
From our Education, values, conditionings.
Underneath there are resonating sensations
with the Living ~ Force of Universal nature.
Seeing a tree, animal, buttercup, butterfly, bird.
Beholding it as a life-form swaying in the wind.
Sacrificing this direct experience for a concept!
'Identifying' ~ this Instant is always here!
We are always One with Now ~
*** Is Life Itself ***
We're believing in apparent reality in our heads.
Believing which programs we are told to do* be.
Seeing it as Frangipani, puffer fish, chameleons.
Any of the myriad species in a Zero energy field.
The Power is in not being*Separated from Now.
A big delusion to think it's there and not here!
That you always have to add more content
to be completed ~ Really need to Identify-
less with content and more with Space.

*

<u>Wake Up!</u>
Cells feeling the Sun ~
Occupying your heart.
We're all in it together.
"I had my girl on my arm"
Turtles laying eggs in the pouring rain;
The Navy turned up and took them all away!
You made it happen! Seeing it from my Palapa.

<u>She Loves Me ~ She Becomes Me.</u>
Mind-Object * Mind-Form ~ My Voodoo Love Doll!
"Form is only a temporary expression of the Whole"
Unconscious people don't get it ~
You can't have My Life, Me & Myself.
You can Un/Create whatever you want.
'MY LIFE' ~ YOU ARE LIFE * ITSELF!
No Separation of an Ego*Mind* Processor!
"Let's chop all the trees in the ancient, sacred wood!"
TRIES TO FEEL THEY'RE A *PART * OF LOVE

*

<u>Same Respect Frequency</u>
In the Jungle the Lionesses hunt.
They'll kill for him * Alpha Male!
Feelings with No Attachments.
~ Awareness Is Consciousness ~
She knew exactly what she was doing.
Cold hearted, crashed the car into the dead sea.
Twisted your heart & you're drowning in self misery!
You treated me as if I Never Existed ~ not as your great lover!
Can't you see, 'In this multi*dimensional Cosmos it's All Love?'
Then she left without another word ~ Stars Shooting from Heaven!

*

<u>Karma*Karma*Karma*Panorama</u>
You are what you are ~ You're Creation
Creator of your own Magic Kingdom sutra.
You are what you do there ~ ask the I Ching.
You are your own Healer ~ To Love Yourself.
You need to go through what you got to go through,
to see its Reflection in you ~ Loving your Eternity.
Know you are expressing your Karmic planes ~
And letting it go with LOVE

She Is Pure Natural Viagra Idealisation!

I've let her go, her free will, so now it's up to the Universe ~
Love can be the most Obsessional Illusion in time & space.
Remove the Mind which makes Life too serious; It costs!
Made a problem out of it ~ relinquish it ~ it all comes to you.
Not that it matters anymore they're ultimately all distractions.
The Identification I realized was nonsense*Can't find a solution over
my Mind! "It's never too late to start to begin living that frequency ~ "
"When I grew up the World was Infinite Now it's become Finite!"
Swimming in liquid sunshine knowing Love is Unconditional.
Dreaming beyond the nature of duality (y/our own reality).
Shifting Collective Consciousness "Did I ever tell you
about MY Hell!?" Peeling Everything Off!

*

Love Mannequins Deep in Space

Into the Sun to a Magical Island called AMORE.
I Love Duality ~ Blondes & Brunettes, double D.
You'll need a Heart Transplant! Mr. ...
Life Is Spiritual ~ Ask your Literary Therapist.
A soul mate * Is Live*Space
Done & dusted, forgotten dumped in a gutter of 'non existence'
Are you still able to look up and wonder at the Moon after that?
Melted memories into wax dummies don't blink no time for Anything
Me, I followed my heart

*

Little Ego Demons

We become Separate....
Forgotten who Killed my secret enemy ~
'Good things happen to good people'
Life Is Enlightened by Itself
Seeing into a pool of love.

Cellular Feelings* R *Us2

Addicts need to get the rush of what they're craving chemically!
Loving in anticipation of getting their fantasies fulfilled in ekstasis,
that they are more addicted to! ~ "I can't pimp her out, I'm afraid!"
They're fully Conditioned cortex ~ You'll get it when you are there;
Biochemical * fulfilling peptides! Helps you dance and be as One.

*

You are Life

You only know what you really got when everything is gone!
FREE*DOM TO FEEL ~They can survive on virtually fuck all!
Nothing to lose, no attachment, no inheritance, happy & poor.
It's all Ego without Truth ~ Surrendering into the Emotional Field.
Acceptance, listening to the perfect cacophony not resisting it.
Trapped in an Economic delusional nightmare! Demonic Mass-
Media ~ Channels; Realising we are bigger than the Pain, Slave!
Cosmic Consciousness ~ Bio*whole grain Organic Consciousness.
We perceive, transmit, receive, experience through the 'Mind-set'
A Vast Zero Space being reduced into just an 'Object'....
As defined ~ not the synergetic, Quantum*Universal field!
The delusion is the Separation of themselves ~ from
Holistic, whole beingness * Eternal Cosmic existence.
It all changes in this World when people are feeling
Loving empathy ~ overriding with all Forgiveness.
Look Inside your own Temple.

*

Fabricating Thrones

It's all a 'Game of IN*FORMATION' ~ All shapes & Sizes *
What you look at is not as important as how you are feeling.
Awareness of your Present nature * Awareness in the Silence
Stillness within ~ only Feeling Itself as there's No Real 'Object'.
Walking with an entity, Mentality, Mind-created Self called ME.
Taking Full Possession!

Full Potential

Convincing yourself we're living*beaming in Pure Love Temples.
If you don't give a plant what it needs it doesn't reach its fullness!
'The question, "Who am I" has no answer in consciousness and
therefore helps to go beyond consciousness' Nisargadatta Maharaj
All goes into Ego's feeding Machine, transcends by Consciousness.
Touch it, fuck it, see it, hear it, smell it, taste it, feel it all ~
The physics of passion, desire, lust, fear, hate, anger, love.
Steaming molecules dripping out of her mouth, gotta rub her!
Letting her genie out of the pot into the fire * the Violet flame.
Rising together to heavenly paradise.

*

You Came to Me

Do you realise the concept of a balanced Conscious Mind to start with?
After picking up the pieces of your broken heart what are you left with?
Why would I hate you ~ twisting in the knife of deeper revelation?
A higher reflection shining in the light, burning, suffering in the night.
'I am still in your heart', lovely now please leave me alone as you've
been doing so perfectly ~ not to be in the spirit of hiding the Truth.
Yoni door back to Earth, trapped in wild desire for another rebirth.
Addicted to y/our brain's emotional, chemical, hormonal orbiting.
"I might have a bit of bliss coming"

*

"I Love Screamers!"

Killing time waiting for my girlfriend exploring other opportunities ~
She's not coming she's detoxing and doing her own Astrology chart!
I've an Alien on my back tampering with the remote control; ATTACK!
The Cinderella Armored Tank * the Unicorn*Coconut Rocket launcher,
Ariel's nuclear sub-marine fleet ~ Trembling in front of the Black Sun!
How much of Global economies is squandered on the Military Industries?
REALISE W E A P O N S Are Made For D E S T R U C T I O N!!!!!!
Crimes Against Humanity keeping most people in poverty and starvation!

Satsang Receptor

Perspector*Allowing y/our heart to surf ~ the Universal Space.
It's all a biochemical lesson*realizing duality loving the bliss.
To begin with do you have a sense of an equanimous mind?
If you shit, dream, fuck under a coconut tree you might get
a coconut on your head. After picking up all the pieces of
your broken heart what are you left with? It's **be here now** ~
Just being a peptide or worrying about all that can go wrong!
Let it go, it's just this ~ not infatuated with her golden ass.
Addicted to our emotional Highs * can't let her go again!
Falling in Love ~ over a cascading waterfall
bringing all of it into light consciousness.
Transcending the Illusion of all illusions.
If you want forgiveness, I forgive you.
The choice to leave the dark behind.
Let relations be your Sat Nav!

*

Sentimental Implantologist

Revving my moods like fuck, I couldn't even get it into first!
Even Ignorance is Illusion ~ you give it up to a Higher Bliss.
Knowing you are it, in it, dreamt it, through it, out of it ~ IT'S
Zero Space, disclosing what was invisible underneath the Truth.
How big a gate do you need to keep these Holy caste cows out?
Your perception ~ Godly the Divine is manifested in its reflection
from where do you want to see it, which corner of Mind's Reality?
Feeling the gentle touch ~ of someone going through your PAIN!
That's why we're in Goa to be uplifted sharing joyful soul*energy.
Delightful moments sitting with Beedi Maharaji at the chai shop.
Always another way around the door * Live all your inspiration.
Don't be Attached if you don't want Sensational*PAIN Babe!
"I can only say that from my experiences......

Holographic Oyster Expression
Focus on the Silence (still, alive energy)
Your Awareness & Consciousness ~
Just looking out, same as at any age.
My heart is OPEN ~ the Nature of Real Love.
Doesn't depend on ME, MINE, POSSESSING!
D * e * lusional people becoming Possessed
by their own mental content! "I love real Pearls."
Stored up Emotional PAIN of the Masterful EGO.
Not knowing what we're doing in hate & anger!
An Evil Spirit ~ only the Ego saying, Me & Them.
~ YOU LOSE THAT LOVE OF TOGETHERNESS ~
The Formless in you is the same Formless as in all things.
"Your Mind is your servant not your Master of your true self"
Exploding a Heart Grenade inside Aphrodite's Chateau!

*

On Wounded Knees
"I'm a Pagan Hippie ~ We don't take sides!"
"Where's the medication?" High altitude fruity charas;
Pills anybody? "Give me Infatuation not any limitations!"
"I take my prescription and my thoughts & moods change"
Moneyfested, Art of Living ~ touched by the same wavelengths.
He's a walk-in wizard from the Pleiades, MDMA in the water ~
K the new Heroin, a sedative for the masses giving Absolution.
Mesmerized in Jerusalem, sent a squad of Ninja headhunters.
"You've been warned!" 'From this point nudity is Obligatory'
Living our Potential allowing us the Freedom to transmute.
On an Atomic Level*Particles colliding*Quantum entanglement*
Once they've separated they continue resonating at same frequency
& same time ~ hemispheres in balance ~ hearts in equilibrium.

Docking Onto Her * Invoking Eros'* Ejaculations!
Plants & Trees Give Life! Mother Earth as Super*Beingness.
People are Self's Consciousness ~ of Spacious Awareness.
They just can't see Consciously * Realization that we are it!
"I am an energetic seed of Cosmica loving all that's Life"
Chained himself naked to the top of the Monsanto building.
"If you hold onto concepts then you are bound by them"
Allowance is letting you fall into Super Consciousness ~
Going to a higher rebirth ~ connecting the Crystallites.
The more you ground yourself the higher you can fly.
You are the vehicle to hold this frequency of energy.
Aligning the fields ~ going to the transcendental*self.
Letting go of your 'Self-Ego' ~ Conditioned Id/entity.
Vibrations of Acceptance seeing yourself on that Plane.
Don't judge yourself; You are your only Judge, be here now!
On a different channel, feeling frequency, then you are Free.
Experiencing the Eternal Power of Cosmic Purity in you
Unfolding Inner Peace and harmony

_*_

What's goin' on?
Question one: 'When is a Demon not Demonic?'
"It's murder Baba, killed those people unfairly!"
Seeing the Insanity, who's not totally Insane?
Consciously Conscious the End goal; 'I'm still Alive'
Super happy just before delirium, wobbly in your brain
So identified with the thoughts; "I am F.... very angry!"
A light Inside ~ Turning up, turning down, switch Open.
Accepting the beauty of it all coming & going ~
Space in your heads is empty without thinking.
I'm into Drama Queens; Not in front of my shop!
Coming out from the Space inside.

Life Is Consciousness

Getting deeper, going Higher ^ knowing it all in the ashes ~
True teaching is being empty, opening for that, coming from
S U P R E M E * C O N S C I O U S N E S S
N O T S P I R I T U A L E G O ID ENTITY
'The Mind can't Comprehend F O R M * LESS * NESS
Has to make it into an O B J E C T > A GOD, YOUR GOD!
*F O R M L E S S * E N E R G Y ** Everywhere It's* L I F E*
Listening to Silence you're seeing/feeling the **Life** Inside You.
Conscious Attention Is Space ~

*

'Love' s * Communication breakdown

How to fuck someone unsuspecting in the back!
"I Love gushing Sultanas, dripping into my mouth.
Languid intimacy ~ moving through blissful ecstasy.
"I'm too cool for my satellite, crystal*lite Space suit"
Hot Sun beams warming your Great balls of fire.

*

Obsessive Compulsive Compliance ~ Free Spirit

Recalibrating not justificating nor more Pontificating!
Burning all my sorrows in a chillum kiln ~ the balance,
light as a feather * Drowning in the embers of my disbelief!
Crystalline Dopamine ~ evaporating the tortured & confused mind man!
'Kill a cow in Haryana get bail, rape in the Punjab get bail, murder a Dalit
in India get bail, caught with LSD. in Goa get 10 years in jail and No bail!'
You believe it ~ concept of loyalty, honoring the memory and won't let go;
"Even if I torture myself to the end!" Let it go ~ Observe the still Bodhi tree.
Inspiration of a 'Weeping Woman' & 'I locked myself up in an Asylum' series.
Bending light around other dimensions ~ 'I am Tantric Magic by the Chorten'

"She was a Cruel Torturer!"

Met her in an Underground Cannabis club with her Love buds*
budding wet! "I'm happy if people are Happy" You Enjoy it do it.
Reflections of Equality ~ we're humans, let's be that Please!
We were going to a Swingers' Pagan festival of Polyamory;
And consciousness will get You here now

*

Her Fig Jam

Have to give yourself more Free LOVE ~
More Consciousness, Self worth, Respect.
Doing it with LOVE * I don't know what I am;
I don't know who I am because I AM * I * Om * It.
Real Intelligence is more than Intelligence we invent.
Chemicals singing to chemicals * I find in my hippocampus

*

Made to go through 'Cold Pussy!'

Looking for Love with a rare Jungle honey ~ Can't go wrong!
I've been to Infinity, ending of an extremely Romantic love story.
"One day this war will be over and I can return to my love poems"
First see it on the inside then you can create her on the outside ~
Soul mate Kaleidoscopes coming together in one synchronistic instant.
Waking up from a hallucinogenic dream, Love is a drug ~ come down!
Eventually You have to die to your expectations each & every moment.
Yeah when they're not trying to fuck you ~ Transmutating ourselves!
Throwing myself at an Indian woman's feet, begging for a blessing!

*

Psychedelic Asylum * Trance Ashram

Deeper Emotional * Attachments in the Miracle * grow bag.
Lines of Cocaine & Opium ~ the next Orgasm Obsession!
Avatars driving to Oblivion without a care in their Minds.
No girl in the Tantric harem who doesn't want to be there.
"I forgot where I put my list!"

Fringe Conspiracy Hippies.

Iceland did it! Threw out all the ingrained crazy Capitalist corruptionistas!
The System's got to go ~ worrying about the Chaos; Give 'em Gateaux!
Who is loving this Corporation Identified, Globalism gone 'Uber MAD?
"We recognize now that it was Wrong!" Give Sleeping Beauty a kiss!
Sold their Souls, born on a cross in a morass; The Sun God's comin' back.
'We are the light * All One light'
We're it experiencing Cosmic.

*

That's What Happens

"All the bullets turned to fleeting butterflies" Machine guns into sculpture!
Focus on the best possible outcome ~ Full of singing birds, 'tweet, tweet'.
"I gave all my girlfriends freedom and they all fucked off with another man!"
A Python invisibly crossing the floor, "I still love you, I forgive you really!"
"If you got a harem you gonna write a lot of romantic, erotic poetry"
Moving into Rumi's pleasant, refreshing, inspirational Rose garden.
Darling you don't exist in my life anymore, it's as you wanted it to be.
Everything's hooked up to the machine, it's never enough what they do!
She's not coming she's detoxing; Stay calm and take more Psychedelics!

*

Dissociated ~ Vibes

Conditioned to see nihilistic content ~ just dream my dream.
Looking for Singularity ~ the Real movie; Cultural Inventions.
She was a Ketaminite and Ideological casualty. Picturesque
creates an Image from 'Reality' devaluing the Real essence.
Things are happening, "If it can't be Now it'll be never & forever!
Going through a DMT warping, having sex in another dimension
Dropping through a hairy wormhole ~ no time to think about it!
Diamonds from Atlantis sparkling in her pierced fairy ring navel.
Life smiles ~ its energy dancing in my heart.

The Divine is in your Heart

I was meant to catch that same midnight train to Georgia Baby!
Raw Choc peptide Brain. CBD enhancers; When it goes Live!
That means more of the BLISS * chemical, wet lips to lips ~
We have to Love each other, imprinting condition in the heart.
You really can't think for another person even for you darling!
It's not in y/our Control, in reality either you do or you don't ~
No more contact with each other, keep a Spiritual connection?
Karma always from the past; Painfully helps us to transcend.
They're situations, fully identifying with 'Objects' in the field.
How far down do you go before it SNAPS; All falling to bits!
Your baggage following you around if you want it to or let go.
"A fuck is just the cherry on the cake I want the whole gateau!"
Virtual reality*You meet & fall in Love on the same wavelength.

*

A Religious War

Children in the Insane Asylum
Starving and covered in flies.
A Religious Madness.
In a hospital full of Tragedy.
A casualty of Truth.
& They're selling us
'Lifestyle & Leisure'

*

Maya's Sisters

Why you don't need Temples.
'KALI is in every woman ~'
"Woman when she's lost the plot!"
It's why you don't want to arouse her.
Time/Life/death ~ People get Soulless, Ego.
Equality of Goddesses without inflated hoods!

Nettle Aliveness

You doin' it all with Love there is No bad Karma.
Attention is Not separate ~ another Life-Form.
Reflecting my Real * Self of Life essence
Recognising ~ Life in All Forms of Gaia.
Existence is Temporary ~ Manifestation!
The mistake we make is believing
the thoughts in our head are for ever ~
'A brilliant state to be in ~ Not knowing'
What we need we can Never know
Because We Are It.

*

You can choose your Love

You own your possessions only when you give them away
or they're owning you. Their main program is to live in shit!
Christ in a Crystal in our heart * shines in all kind of rays.
Free will, life and death in between is drama, is breath!
A big collection of many Stars experiencing life on Earth.
Have to let the other go ~ otherwise it's not Love darling!
Every night the Angels are coming, tuning the visible mask.
Breathing Unconditional LOVE ~ Inhale Peace * exhale Love.

*

Being*here*now

It is what it is and if it's not what it was and you're depressed then….
Everyone does this OM ~ has to learn from this experience as a Soul.
Going through this holy shit; It's just another cleansing!
Looking for 'Live culture' Masters ~ being Present
Appearing ~ resonating in the moment…
Open to Surrender what does it mean?
From over Your Love to All as One ~
Stepping in a bio feedback Universe

Mesmerized Business Model!
"Come in get an egg on toast anytime you wanted!"
He likes the Geisha experience, why wouldn't you?
Life is fragile for those who don't conform to Rules.
Insatiable maniacs, "If they can't control us they'll kill us!"
Food shortages, Abuses of Power ~ disharmony of Stuff.
Many love the interbred Nazi Queen but nobody knows why!
Don't let your kids watch it.

*

'Love Is All'
We experience the personal love as a body/mind 'creation' which is fine
if we are Conscious of how the Mind feeds us dreams, wants, illusions
desires, fears etc and so not to be disturbed by these but keep a sense of
Awareness realising these emotional games are just an 'Object not our true
self and not the Unconditional Love containing all life's feelings*No negativity,
no positivity, values identified in our Mind; Just LOVE itself*Osho said 'it's not
a question of being in Love with someone, it's a question of being Love' ~
Love is authentically inside each of us ~ Once its essence is recognised
it is our birthright to share and be blissful

*

FORMLESS GOD SONATA
'The thought has the person rather than the person having a thought.'
Then you can Play, you see that the FORM IS all an ILLUSION.
We are the Whole of Creation ~ making You Conscious now.
Hypnotised, mesmerized, possessed by insane Egoism.
Generating Ignorance, doubt, reacting Unconsciously.
Someone in authority has a thought and pronounces!
She told him all kinds of lies, fearful demon thinking.
Exotic Aliens are just a load of other 'Object-Forms"
Truth's Essence Is ~ Can't make it into an Object.
Meditation as an 'Object of desire' ~ not going
beyond Perceptions, 'Need for Enlightenment'
His Spirit was singing & dancing within hers!

<u>Feeding the Form of the Egoic!</u>
Unconditional ~ Love comes from in You
Stroking a purring pussy catalyser & lovin' it.
Love is not from some thing - a Self-Centred 'Object'
All to do about Nothing ~ Deep unhappiness, Things a waste of Time!
You observe it, seeing IT not seeing YOU ~ Un*Identifying it in Silence.
Ego wants to judge everything; A good servant not your Master mate!
These Thoughts are running our lives ~ real fulfillment is beyond it in*stilled.
'Turned out the driver of the van was a father just taking his kids to school.'
All Killed by Apache Helicopters; Committing War crimes, Systematic tortures!
'Enhanced Interrogation Techniques' Made it legal, Crimes Against Humanity!
Mental Form, Emotional body, energetic fields, dualistic-attachment, Insanity!
Thinking that this is/n't Really happening ~ feelings extreme in y/our Mind.
Telling the Unconscious voice in our head to "Shut the f…. up!"
This situation is there for us to learn how to fully Surrender to
the feeling, to transcend ~ this 'Object-Mind' Altar Ego state.
*

<u>At Bar Ayahuasceros</u>
It's a Master witness of time ~ *)*
Need some Silent Meditation becoming
Stillness Inside ~ Need some Sun * Light
radiating a flowering stream of Consciousness.
Until you drop the Attachment…
It's only feeding all the Senses!
The feeding Mind needs to keep on mooching ~
Changing, being Alive…. 'Closed Eyes Scenic'
"I know more why you fucked me than you do!"
"And I know nothing really, accept to truly forgive"
Listening to a barking dog as if in a Cezanne tableau.

'Conscious Segregation' ~ Feeling It Flee
Be One no Separation of Ego your anger can burn it up, You're Free
Art of War put all the treasure away! What's a Massacre mean dad?
The Psychic messenger is also a channeling Conceptual Artist, so am I!
4th dimensional bridge to Unconditional Love leading us to blissfulness
In your being Love ~ to being One with everyone in SPACE.
Plasma light from Heaven ~ one streaming with Mother Earth.
Bighting through ~ talking to them as a normal Person!
"Can you see that Comet from the Pleiades mate?"

*

*LSD*Sacred Geometry*Awareness*
A crack in the egg/a different experience.
Taking the natural Super * Conscious trip.
Being Inside fluttering up all her beautiful chakras!
Stars in Space seen as 'Objects' in the Universal sky.
Not realising this Space, forgotten our Cosmic Subject.
'YOU CAN'T FIGHT LOVE' ~ REALLY!
Completely overtaken by the inner vibration ~
Power to transmute on their own humane level.
Stay Present and everything that happens is a Gift!
It's this energetic Consciousness that really matters.

*

Shaved Pussy Darshan
Showing them a bit of Magic
And they start to believe!
Just go with your feeling ~
Love is when you are Conscious.
All in One * over the Soul * Spirit
****Same * Space****
Trusting in that again
finding it in Yourself.
Walled up in China!

In the Osmosis Moment

Thinking will she like it or not? Are You Really, Really Worth It?
Not intended to be taken seriously but obviously the Mind does so!
Like talkin' to yourself the words keep on coming, keep repeating!
Going in Circles, Spirals; Feeling the Power in your listening to it!
You can never really Know IT as It's beyond the Finite Mind.
Our limited brain can't comprehend the FORMLESSNESS.
Mental * Emotional 'Object' dreamed up in true Zero Space.
Look at the way your own Mind works, on a Rollercoaster!
You have a natural breath ~ make it Conscious.
Don't need Synthetics, ultimately Life is in Itself
All Loved Up Naturally.

*

Touching ~ an Ethereal, Remorseless Beauty Queen!

A set of variations ~ I'm in your Love frequency my Sweetheart.
Tele*transportation ~ Sensational flight to Venus' heart of bliss.
Soul waiting until it finds a body, learning about her desires!
Looking out & perceiving the World as 'Subject' not 'Object'
The Consciousness you gave yourself ~ Trusting the light.
Sweeping the streets with fulfillment, open to it, very Zen.
Shape-Shifters, cold blooded, no empathy, no feelings.
Not satisfied with Earthly pleasures ~ outer vibrations.
They can't do anything if you have Trust in Yourself.
If they go in the feeling mood they lose Control!
Chased by reptiles, Fear mongers, Men in black!
Squatted by homeless veteran WW11 soldiers.
Human's Crash! "I fell in love with a Tiger!"
"If you see yourself as two you're fucked!"
Becoming One in the Soul ~ feeling it.
Love duet's * deep Intimate Exposure.

<u>'The Dragon Depression Lakes'</u>
In sadness & in health 'til death us do part~For ever & Never, Celebrate life!"
Their job is to suck cocks and they all love it! Experiencing Hieros Gamos.
Gave her a throbbing sparkly diamond, she gave me a twinkle in the eye.
Bend over beauty, business in heat! Your destiny is in this moment.
It's Real ~ She doesn't want to give it me back.
You become a Soul, giving up your personality.
First doing All the Illusions with my Devotee.
Take responsibility for what you have.
You find the true Master in Yourself.
You give that Love No-Ego Identity.
Being in the 'Allowance' to go Up.
In the game ~ being the Observer.

*

<u>Lips to Lips Adoration</u>
It's All about Love ~ Not Co-dependence of the Spirits' need.
'Namaste' chica seeing the soul in everyone and its reflection.
Devotional Love giving it all up to a higher frequency ~ freely.
Daily stuff gets taken care of, Concentration, focus on Yourself.
ASPECT ~ To let go of the 'EXISTENTIAL FEAR' who said that?
When you Know ~ you're being taken care of in violet flames.

*

<u>Drug Void</u>
First I had to have my own experiences of Buddha's lessons.
Filling a hole of enchantment with recreational enhancements.
Not many Social, Spiritually Conscious people around ~
'Insanity Rules' anything you want to add to that?
No Soul discerning between what is right or wrong!
Unconscious People dropping bombs on different Temples.
"I don't go for money I go for sweet eternal honey"
The Happening ~ 'What Was is No More'

Sold Souls Souk
'A Meteor they believe is a stone sent from their invisible God'
"There is Nothing to Fear except for Ignorant Fear itself"
Business' No heart ~ Asking for the energy to come in.
Everyone for themselves can't do it for someone else!
Making it for Yourself, making it visible in Golden rays.
You can only give it away when you know you own it.
Not dependent on it, not obsessed watching it in Fear.
Make it REAL ~ the Processing, giving You an Imprint.
'It has You as its Slave ~ In the Mind-setting'
Free Souls cultivating real Loving Kindness.
*

Thrashing Revenge!
Myth of Leila in a mini micro string, rampaging illusions!
Crashed onto the white crystal rocks, it's All a Mind game.
Aware of the naked senses, conscious, seeing You Are ~
Watcher of that dream, first you have to discern that game;
Which is not your body it is nothing only another delusion!
Make distance*Soul is the Imprint of God who makes You.
*

Be One with It
North Korea all in Uniform takes away Your sense of Self.
We need to be Conscious of our own Conscious self.
It has You as its Slave ~ in your Mind-Set
Their Love revolves around all their Fears!
Insecurities, expectations, desires, Controls,
bondages against Love's Magic * melting in it.
You're giving it to yourself, don't even Judge it!
The thief, avenger, rich, poor, wife, priest, S/elf.
When you see this as Theatre then you are Free.

Soul to Soul Love

The whole personality doesn't matter anymore ~
You love the Soul of someone, how to not come out of it?
Soul to Soul connection ~ multi*dimensional frequency.
Our unique imprint ~ karmic drops in the Ocean
Breathing through what you thought Conditional.
The emotions are just the flowing
Mind ~ substance of the feelings.

*

The Total Show

"One candle to light a whole cave" ~ She is a Solar Satellite.
Many have lost their Souls, don't know what they're doing!
'It is what it is' ~ looking inside the Open energetic Space.
I Am Fuel not collateral damage burning in this razed field.
Coming to Your self ~ not making sense on the outside now.
You see what you want to see how can I judge? Trust to Rust!
Going through many Portals & dimensions at the same time ~
Coming from the heart ~ empowered frequency best reflection.
Connected to OUR Mother Earth ~ trusting in it completely
Her beingness

*

Sniffer Cat

"I walked away from loads of bad debt!"
'Metro boulot dodo'… as big as a Lion.
Capitalism's fascism gone MAD; No one really knows.
Going off-grid now ~ had a long conversation with a Porcupine!
Stuck right in the chest with a quill, real diamonds in her slippers!
Finally got it and destroyed it; Don't need any torch, it's all glowing.
It's important to climb out of the grave ~ try a trip down the Orinoco.
Just to show me she's had enough ~ the extreme is always lurking about!
Can't hide the Truth seeing through the wheel ~ Love your f....g neighbor!
Putting it into practice; Caring for the Life ~ Living in the Oneness.

Le Grand Guignol
Allowing Yourself to be TRUE to Oneself
Omnificent*Omnipresent*Omniconscious*Omnipotent*Om
He's totally owned by this belief in being POWER * FULL!
Falling in Love seems needing, security, a rock in a storm.
A big Duality ~ game, ultimately showing us we're All One.
Giving Energetic blessings more than Materialistic FORM.
Nature is Divine, Love's fulfillment, what holds it all together!
Our Ego must die ~ in flow not working Against one another.
Knowing we are ONE ~ Trusting together with no Attachment.
To hold onto the old picture has No Sense anymore; You left!
Still in duality going through the Karma with more Awareness.
You eat and you shit ~ an Organic process happens in Space.
We get fractalised and see the crystallized World in that light.
Soul to Soul with devotional, equanimous, unconditional Love.
No more Ego giving it up to the Creator ~ working through You.
Reflections in you making us Happy * You are my Gift of LOVE

*

Ask an Angel
Deep in Space
Deep Love in Space

*

Venus *Aller Retour
Your Ego's reasoning overpowered your Heart.
I'm in a vacuum, if you don't remember!
what's the fucking point of being in love?
Bewitched Space * My Love is Eternal.
I'm very happy to meet you.
How deep do you want to go ~
How good is your true Telepathy;
Are you able to cross the Cosmic sea?
Being in adoration ~ timelessly with me.

104

It Looks Bigger than It Is!!

Attention somewhere else * thoughts somewhere else.
Consciousness is Not affected by what is happening.
Conceptual values "I am standing in a queue & happy"
Determined by your breath ~ Love in the Space IN/around them.
Stillness and Presence, that was all effortless fulfilling your purpose.
Bringing in Consciousness, Love, bliss whatever is, 'Sat Chit Anand'
SHOCK! It has to come from You it can only come from You; Simple.
I've been to Venus and back with her! * LET YOUR LIGHTS SHINE *

*

Spinning Surya!

Cosmic dancing ~ Sun rising * Sun setting, her Vulva Moon glistening.
You got it all goin' on Inside you ~ standing in a queue not lost the plot,
seeing it with LOVE not what's apparently happening in our imaginations.
Seeing the holistic forest as nature's source or only a resource to exploit?
Identity from the heart ~ letting In/divi/dualistic Mind go ~ out into the ether.
The Stillness not the accelerated Ego vibe disasters, taken over by the mob.
Listening to a voice in our Mind most of our lives that doesn't want to STOP!
Why keep repeating thinking of these FORMS * try embracing its nothingness
The Sun is always shining, Cosmos is expanding; It's a bit too bright for them!
Crossing through eternal Multiverses ~ Aligning with Unconditional Love * GO!

*

'No Closer to the Truth'

Breathe in the light ~ out the dark.
Feeling the natural rhythm of Life ~ expand, contract.
Tides comin' in & goin' out ~ up and down, round & round.
Concepts of 'Spiritual' Projects 'Objects' in people's Minds.
All Objects are duality ~ Conjuring more Ego FORM Limits.
Attention is Formless ~ with no 'Object of Itself' defined in Space.
Vertical not 3D Linear dimensions ~ Time in Form changes, birth, death
'Be happy don't allow the situation to determine your state of consciousness
but allow your state of consciousness to determine the situation ~.

Hallo Palau

Naked girls with flowers in their hair ~ natural beauties.
Good lungs, free diving for real Pearls in Neptune's bed.
*Just there Not thinking this or that * Breathing the light.*
Consciousness only the Present ~ All You'll ever Know!
"To breathe or Not to breathe?" Pure breath, Prana life.
"I'm making the choice to breathe in this Space of Light"

*

His Feeling of False Identity

It All matters ~ making things serious in Your Own Mind is Hell.
Violence & Ignorance to strengthen his, her own Ego over You!
Vibrations of Joy respecting the other Consciously, generously.
Where People Are So Separated ~ losing this Sense of being.
"In the walled garden, is that the place to add things?"
Heaven is where it doesn't matter ~ Becoming Lighter.

*

How I Feel Inside

The Mind can't comprehend that with No beginning or End;
Beyond judgment of any FORM, recognizing God is All Life.
They only Think it's of 'Objects' ~ forgetting Consciousness.
Ego playing to take y/our Attention away from it in you.
We make the Limits ~ Mind is judging all the time.
Manifesting Infinite Forms to Know Itself!
Formless everything existing in its Space.
London, Delhi, Goa, Here is where I AM ~
Walking down any street, having FUN.
Just reacting to the thought Procession
by a Mental entity created by the Mind.
All Life is seen through that.
'This Pill melts your fat'
Formless energy within.

You've been Mullahed & Muftied!
You're happy with the Sun, girls, someone giving herself Love.
"You can't give/accept/share Love if you don't Love Yourself"
No expectations ~ no one knows what will come next.
All Ego & Judgment, 1st thing the Mind wants to do!
Just look at her cellular Cosmos get the feeling.
No duality no separation see what it is, healing.
Disidentify otherwise you're POSSESSED.
A mad thought telling someone to Kill!

"Faites l'amour, pas la guerre!"
"You Shine Your Light"
In the Present ~

*

Each one is Life ~ Living force
for realizing Consciousness in itself
No thinking just lookin' with Awareness of....
A Conditioned thought process ~ Mental+Form!
Feeling your heart ~ Is not Interpreting Space

*

What do you Desire?
'Che sera sera', SAY AFTER ME ~ "I am Free!" 'Inshallah'
If this is Globally accepted as 'Normal' then what the f...
does a Tyrannical dictatorship look like to Mr. Raif Badawi!?
Execution's not the Solution! They're Demons and have to go!
She's raped by 7 men & received 6 months in Jail & 200 lashes!
Coming from the heart ~ empowered by Soul's rising frequency.
We have the best reflection ~ connected through Mother Earth.
May have lost their Truth, don't know what they're doing.
Trusting it completely ~ Its beingness, its Humanness!
No more Ego ~ give it up to the Creator.

Never Rehabilitated

'His name is engraved on the wall of the prison'
"There's more to this war than meets the eye!"
Executed at the University ~ say no more!
Most of her family died during the famine.
Beheaded on Friday, "They're feeding themselves
on our changing emotional bodies" You know who!
Losing ourselves they're eating that energy Chaos.
Going into Inner Peace don't fall into their dualities ~
Breaking the Cycles, where is your Mars and Venus?
Unfold out of the garbage * 'OM MANI PADMA HUM'

*

Nothing Adds Up

Oxygen amplifies light ~ Shrapnel hit the maternity ward!
Sun's dancing in a blood-stained, black hole theory of Chaos.
Keep realising Consciousness ~ to see another Sun* rise.
Sufis understand human weakness & deep forgiveness;
Not the fundamental threats of Sin from a grand Mufti!

*

Creative Energy

Go down to take someone up and lift yourself too ~ 'Om Mani Padma Hum'
Undoing the knots in the net of Ego ~ Shiva the Destroyer chilling in Fiji!
Cosmic energy not Cosmetic surgery. Wiser than an elephant!
Heart attraction to giving the Blessing in Spirit.
"No one can ever live your Life besides You"
Emotion as music spinning in your ear drums.
Harmonic OM ~ Transmuting the DNA strands to Shangri-La.
Balanced the battery with new life ~ Surrendering to a new day.
From where we learn to become Unity in this, dancing Cosmic frequency.
Being together in One, all up to us, trust to trust again ~ Unattached to it.
"Every day 24/7 is Ramadan in lots of Africa, brother!" ~ "Inshallah"

<u>Scalar Waves to Violet Flames</u>
Loving ourselves, they're not allowed, afraid to think.
Informed bringing others over ~ into the hard FORM!
Your Information's being * Bombarded on the front line.
Seeing the light through Unconditional Love ~ ET. friendly;
Mental-Form just another 'Object' in Ultra Spatial Awareness.
Seeing lights from different angles showing us new spectrums.
Partying with Inter*dimensionals everything is always changing!
Going in complete new energy ~ Love Yourself then you can Love.
Soft secrets, everything is Magical * imprints of infinite Divine expanse.

*

<u>A Radical Change of Consciousness</u>
Caterpillar of the Golden light's metamorphosis into a Butterfly.
Learning from the experiences of how they got out of this trap!
In a NWO. Corporate playground ~ Plane debris on the runway!
Just try another Level ~ sharing All in One, accepting each other.
Soul's taken over by Demons ~ Out the cocoon now freer flowing
The Daisy Chain-Gang's Infatuation with Happy Sun-flowers.
A real snake in the grass crying ~ scratch, sniff and spasm!
Crocodile tears all over the prism.
Predators hunting for your Juices.
"Someone needs to end the War!"

**

<u>Crystal Ashram</u>
Land with a mountain's natural spring, treat it Magically.
Brilliant nano-chaos flowing out of the ground fundamentality.
In-formed making the water swirl ~ Revealing itself, I know it exists!
Disciplined density, gravity Stillness ~ Silence sensing what goes on in you.
Your skin, flesh is just a delusion ~ Meditation being the moment right NOW!
All feeling has left the party; There is no limitation dancing Trance together.
Paradise is in you ~ of course it can't be anywhere else can it?
Not in a big ball in the sky or in a Hippy's Spacey Spaceship

It Comes & Goes

Celebrating International women's day; Give her the perfect gift!
Can't go in their own experience trip, shows their betrayal in you.
By putting all the impressions, great memories, it's Not Real.
When you realize this for Yourself, detached You Are Free.
Holding it together over the Love vibration not the 'Object'
Water running through us ~ clearing out our false beliefs.
Being washed away, to know Yourself, is the only Thing;
That is Real*I AM*You are the Creator, Conscious Space.
Free * Love Makes the Picture

*

Etheric Light Frame

Psychic*delicacies helps you Love and be as One.
3D Objectified ~ Interpreted as our Love Life force.
Comet Lovejoy*Orbiting in the Sky ~ inside your 3rd eye.
Aligning her Plasma tail with your Earth and Sun chi energy.
Whatever happens I've got to Welcome it as it's the Present.
Doesn't mean if wealthy they'll be sane never mind Happy!
They drag past into future, don't need Religious conditioning.
Seeing beyond the Veil into our own Cosmic becomings.
"We'll be in the Algarve mate!" "Dropping every day!"
Natural Hanuman on a raw, high THC diet all his life.

*

Through*Energy

You have to experience it to know what it feels like
You have to Allow the Karma we gave ourselves to unfold ~
There are no mistakes only the head judging 'Objects In Space'
In courage coming from the heart and making emotional transmutation.
Opening Portals to different dimensions we're connected to a load of Aliens!
Let the old structure go * not for me anymore ~ it's where the Love comes in.
To be you have to leave hold of those you Love ~ be yourself & Shine out.
A million times higher

Bodhisattva's Share

It's a lie because we're in the flow ~
"You have to lose it to find it"
You are the Ocean's Creator
You have to come from the Inside.
Open channeling letting the energy glow
for the high +ve vibes. 'Vive la Tibet Vive!'
The Pope Is In Despair! Evil Inquisitor come to roost.
They're Not All Megalomaniacs! How do you know?
No feeling of empathy, remorse, cold hearted 'Saint'
Jesuits selling their Souls to this darkest Power!
Just an ugly reflection of the perceived light.
Nothingness * Allness * All in N/one.

*

"I was good at Drama!"

You have to Love ~ Your*Self
Inside to give Loving to the outside.
Otherwise you'll give Pain & Confusion.
Falling into a lovely face * of Trust ~ open Realisation.
Every word is a definition * a beautiful potential Smile.

*

Holographic Visionary

Full Conditionings of Mental-movement ~
Conscious approach to resonance in Oneself.
Trusting in the experience, giving yourself it, surrendering.
Over money vibrations we make ourselves our own Prison!
Openhearted Trip to Sweetwater Lake, at the Banyan tree.
You love ~ you see that you are Loved.
All in One ~ Soul Supremacy*frequency
Because your Spirit is connected to All.
<Integrating the hemispheres of your brain>
Now I'm listening to my own tone ~ becoming

It's just a Phase

The High Lama's diviner eating the prayers.
Mantras stamped out on Om microdots.
"Don't believe that man he's crazy!"
"Go to the Pharmacy and get injections!"
"You landed on the wrong Planet Baba!"
"Don't kill, don't kill the cockroaches!"
Not as effective as flip flops.
"No time to process Fear!"

*

'Notre Dame'

'Religion is for people afraid of going to Hell ~
Spirituality is for those who've already been there.'
Meditating in the middle of a mass of photographers.
Wanting the images to remember why they were here!
Flying still point*Cleansing Harmonic fields ~ It's in Yourself.
You are in the One ~ directing the Consciousness.
Aligning with it all ** to open a new Universal light.
Mango season there'll be a Love-in there.

*

Learning It

We are a fractal of the whole blossoming garden.
A unique pixel in the infinite I*mage that you are.
Working together to make the picture holistic…
Already exactly Perfect as we are.
In our reflection of Ourselves ~ Heartfelt.
'A drop in the Ocean is the whole Ocean'
Shining out of the vibrating Crystal.
Your own breaking of the light.
As You Really want to see it.
Realizing beautiful essence
Inspiration that's All.

We Are It

'Find a Slut' Get Whatsapp numbers; 'Watch these
babes getting fucked hard and losing their Minds!
Acting like real whores, they're just sex maniacs.'
*You are You not the 'Object' * You are the Creator, Oh Yeah!*
Changing our own vibration ~ Allowing it to change inside you.
*Like a Transformer we are channeling Sunbeams * nothing else to do.*
*Transmuting our Mind * Light*workers putting the intent in the E motion.*
Bringing it to Manifestation ~ it's never separated the Alchemic process.
What Spirit is doing with us!

*

The Outlet

Loving the other as Yourself ~ Same same differently.
*One Fractal*Time is eternity*we are just in that Space.*
Let all your Identification, conditioning, judgment go ~
*SURRENDERING ~ When You Are Not **** DIVINE IS.*
Someone made the Connection ~ Not caught up in the Idol
Another Sect 'Object' feeding the Fabulist, let's have respect.
In the Feeling ~ every moment is new, it's up to you....
How you want to Create it ~ A beautiful Conscious
Garden of Divine Delight

*

When She turned her back on me!

*'Be the change you want to see in the World'*Gandhi.*
Responding to your own Heavenly Paradise in Peace
not the cause & effect of Ignorant reactions darling!
Planting deep the common natural human law ~
Bliss balls in the mind & body of a tumultuous Orgasm.
*Sacred Geometry is not Chaos * Christ Consciousness.*
You fall in Love, 'coup de foudre', seeing all the beauty
of the All in One, in her ~ until it changes

Shock Them Awake!

Real Emotions of Sadness that the dream we made is broken!
'Cold Pussy' has to let go of the beautiful feelings of my Addiction.
Not to get caught up in it ~ thinking you're playing a clever game.
Dancing the way you want, Rainbow Warriors bringing light
over translucent bridges ~ People don't want to see themselves!
What a f.....g World we live in, give it up at once to the Divine.
Taking another stepping stone ~ Surrendering into luminescence.
Take away Ego ~ Soul to person, soul to soul, soul to Infinity.
So we realize we are in essence all One

*

All Starts With You

*Can't change the Planet * can only change Yourself ~*
then see the World ~ dropping Your ubiquitous Self-Ego.
What you thought was right or wrong; You lied to Yourself
About her Devotion and you don't want to let the crazy go ~
Allowing the Mind-Control imprints of ourselves to the Max!
Conceptual fall in the flow ~ and be streaming FREE

*

Ungracious Selfish Ego Shell

Seeing through the lies, corruption, deceit, denial and betrayal.
From a Prison of Fear the Goose has flown out the golden egg!
Transmutation is transforming in our own beingness
You realized Consciously what you are ~ A process,
a witness of yourself, of who you thought you were.
*Potential was always there * Power to break the egg!*
Rebirth a new life, You can leave the Trap behind.
Thoughts, words, concepts, feelings lost in Space.
Discover your new imprint for action.
Free will you Create over the Mind.

Transcended Sensations ~ Getting out of it!
*Your Mind telling you a story and your body feeling the emotions ***
They're Unaware of who they are, believing they're an Idea in their head!
*In the absence of sound is Silence ~ Form * less is always, always there.*
*There's a lot of 'maybes' you don't need to Know ~ the Illusionary ***
Thinking it's Mad but it isn't! Is the Sun a Hot or Cold hollow Portal?
"If you tell the child the name of the bird it will never see the bird."
Is it Alzheimer's? No, stay in the simplicity of the Present*here*now.
*Realising your Attention to Space * Is Awareness * Consciousness.*
She's the Space for what happens ~ Not Attachment to what happens
In that Space
*

*No Comparisons ~ All the Possibilities * Not One Dancer*
When you see through the wheel another vision appears.
On a Psychic Level 'When you are healed you are whole'
A point in the middle where you become One in yourself.
Only communicating with his eyes; "They're dying like flies!"
You need the right perspective ~ no need to involve yourself
unless you do. Enjoy yourself in the new, let the Old Mind go.
All explanations, definitions are wrong, you're out of it Now!
Docking into the UFOrbs from her Venusian Vulvastarship.
I'm an ET too on the only Planet that has wars!
You've bound yourself in an Illusion of the Mind.
Out of the Mind ~ the Lotus is blooming in mud.
This is the way we are ~ 'Om Mani Padma Hum'
It's through me that I create my Paradise on Earth.
*Shakti is how it appears * Shiva is the Destroyer.*
Happy to meet you ~ my Love is Eternal.
*Flickers of Universal light * Letting flow go.*
*** Lots of Crystal energies permeating us ***

Spinning Photon Wheel

"Once children were sniffing glue couldn't get glue anymore!"
Seeing through the lies; ~ Viva la Revolution Inside Us.
Allowing yourself to be Free in the Light Plasmagoria.
Bringing it into Contact ~ being sensualness, having it,
giving each the Freedom * being Aware of our Addictions.
Don't go in the negative, don't need to compare with anyone.
Be who you are, Eternal as Spirit ~ Truth Is behind the Veil.
These gateways are Open now to realize our true Potential.
"Each one is a Life ~ Consciousness realizing Itself"
"No thinking just looking with Formless Awareness ~"
Realising a Conditioned thought process ~ Mental-Entity.
Feeling with your heart ~ No Interpretations of Open Space
'The drop in the Ocean diffuses becoming the eternal Ocean'
OMNIPRESENT*OMNISCIENT*OMNICONSCIOUS*OM

*

Extremely Golden Reliquary

"How many Idols can you look at!?"
'STOP THINKING ~ COME TO GOA'
The Light Is shining Inside You Baba.
It's just to be nice with who's
sitting next to you ~

*

Comet Sungrazer

Scalar wave frequencies ~ controlling y/our Mind-sets.
We broke the devil's net and now we can fly out of it ~
Emotional waves ~ time waves*crystal energy comin' in.
Plasma flashing in her hot tail, loaded in alignment to me.
Some are afraid to let go of their shadow ~ out of the dark.
Holding it Consciously as a way of growing symbiosis.
Our higher crystalline Chakras * Starry-lit Osmosis.
Over this Presence your diamond shines brilliantly!

Surrendering
It's the Space of Awareness ~ Is You.
Tuning into the Space Inside You, then
You're resonating with all Cosmic Space.
There's the Love coming from Me, My Ego ~
Believing in the emotions felt by thoughts in your Mind!
'Then there's the Real Love * that's being an Angel'
'You experience Peace ~ then it's good'

*

'Double Dealing'
If You don't know what duplicitous means then you should go look it up!
Let what happens happen, observe the Mind dancing in essential Space.
Embracing everything that comes from around the corner ~ Consciously!
Her Yin in my Mind Is our Awareness * Awakened Happy Together In Love.
'I think of myself as a window frame with the light shining through.' E Toller.
The purpose of life*Space because it's Formless * not filling it with Thoughts

*

Engaging in an Orgy * Testing the Mind-Forms
Underneath the Conditioned Mind, covered by Identities, Mental-movement.
Natural Highs ~ Imagining you are a Beautiful Star from Venus' hot Moon.
"Our Mother Earth is a Temple not a rubbish dump" Om Namah Shivaya.
"'Do not let the behavior of others destroy your inner peace." Dalai Lama.
'The human brain is made up of 100 billion neurons and nearly 100
trillion synapses. There is 300 times more connections in the brain than
there are stars in the Milky way galaxy.' *** See the Resonance Project.
The theatre of Ego Identification, lack of Feelings, worthy of Shakespeare!
Being the Cosmic Subject not the Worldly Object and how it applies to
Consciousness ~ 'To be Conscious of Consciousness or not to be?'
Relationship Box, we mistake the needing, wanting for falling in Love.
Ego blocking you, judging of Being ~ Knowing you are the Space.
"Open the window and let the light shine through."

<u>Mr. Orwell's 'Housewives' Favourite Cookbook'</u>
"In a time of Universal deceit telling the truth is a Revolutionary Act"
'There's nobody there talkin' 'bout, ok let's make Life better for all'
"The cells in your body react to everything that your mind says;
Negativity brings down your Immune System."
In the Mind all your dreams can come True ~ Time flashes by.
Projecting the Future ~ situations; It's Never like you Imagined!
'I've fallen in Love ~ with a thought in my head;' Not the being!
If you're Insane the human Mind totality is accepting it as Reality.
Once you Love you let go of the ego losing the desire & fear duality.
It can't be remembered, something a brain can't ever comprehend!
There's No 'It' as It Is Nothing ~ Form*Less in Essence*light spirit.
Mind can't recognise 'Awareness' It is Thoughtless *Consciousness.
We put FORM > My God, your wife, our king, homeland, Nintendo!
Thinks that Is It when It is Life Itself * Get to the place of just being.
"In Truth there is No Death ~ Life is an ever changing Cosmic Ocean"
I spend most time on the surface just being tossed about in the waves.
We Think that's It and it's all perfectly 'Normal' ~ like accepting Stress!
*

<u>'Global Paradigm Field' *** Spaceship Earth A Living Temple</u>
Fluoride in the water! Our Mind cannot comprehend just SPACE
< The Formless, invisible, anything beyond its limited spectrum >
What in the World are you f.... spraying on us in an Aluminium sky?
Seeding the clouds with Poisons; Trying to protect us from the Sun!
Some Evil doers destroyed the Indian mango crop without telling them!
'HAARP' ~ 'High frequency Active Auroral Research Programming et al.
Secret weapon Weather Warfare, Chemtrails, 'High Energy Liquid Lasers'
With the recognition of a Frame of Mind in a Space of changing Sensations.
"LOVE CAN ONLY COME FROM YOU"

Super Fertile Ishtar!
"If there's no mind there's no desire ~ no fuck-ups!"
"I'll cross that bridge when I come to it!"
"Do you know where I can get any LSD?"
"Spread the Love and Enjoy It"
"Does anyone really think that Bunny rabbits and
Easter eggs have anything to do with the Crucifiction?"
"I don't have a care in the world!" ~ Shantibaba.

*

*A SHOCK * Tumor!*
"The draft is about white people sending black people to fight yellow people
to protect the country they stole from the red people." Muhammad Ali.
'War is when your Government tells you who the enemy is ~
Revolution is when you figure it out for yourself.' On the Inside.
*Nature will look after itself * In Zero Point let go allow it to transmute ~ to be.*
No argument, no standpoint, demands, Self-Identified Illusions from the past.
You can appreciate Feelings of Loss because you can see the Space beyond.
*The World is here to wake us up * Evolutionary flower blossoming Conscious.*
'Love can only come through You' ~ Staying in the simplicity of the here now*

*

Krishna with his Shakti Radha
"Doesn't anyone believe in 'Live and Let Live' anymore?"
'Nuclear power is a hell of a way to boil water' Einstein
Bluefin Tuna and every other fish in the Ocean were poisoned.
Self pity ~ You sent me spinning into a dark chasm darling!
He's having the ecstasy of seeing Divine Light in her.
All just Forms entrapped in desires and fears
the delusions, multi dimensions of your Mind Constructions.
'Realising everyone understands from their own level of perception'
Psychedelic Rock, Slave Dynasty, Heart Grenade, 'Ma detonatrice!'
Exhalation at the Portals of Venus ~ coming to a beautiful end.
It's cool to meditate ~ In trance at the springs of Mons Veneris

119

Unconscious Illumination!
Changing the Illusory Mind-set attaining in the Mental-form reality.
*Not Still ~ feeling the moment now * Not the I know, Identified Ego.*
My Mind, I don't need to Think ~ getting into the natural groove ~
Knowing Things by losing them! Not possessing, judging, Seeing it.
MDMA's good for breaking duality's barriers down ~ of Thought!
"WANNA TAKE YOUR CLOTHES OFF AND DANCE?"

*

Erase Nostalgia
"Remembering her won't bring you any bliss, not getting another kiss!"
*We are multi*dimensional * give Blessings and it makes you Free*
Genetic Solar Dynasty King evolving from a translucent jelly fish!
What's important is the last blink ~ of Happiness or Sadness.
He's the personal secretary to the Lord of Death, playing back
your Akashi record ~ No more birth is a pattern in their dream.

*

'Today Coke Is King'
'Love is the absence of judgment' ~ Dalai Lama.
"I prefer sex than violence; They're f…. mad!"
Light is piercing through a slit in her blinds!
"That's why it's a Big hit in India; Girls love it"
And that's why they banned it, Meow meoooow.
Baking on it; Get yourself a Special K. haircut too!
*The Universe is made of Chemicals * It's how you ~*
twist & turn them together creating something from it.
Which God do Japanese worship? Nintendo, Butoh, Banzai!
Grew Mango and Coconut Bonsai trees with their fruit in Osaka!
"It makes you very sensuous to the touch ~ a bag of Meow & K.
*in your pocket with MDMA; Angel Dust * Divine, passionate lust!"*
Cobra energy shooting up ~ standing on its tail and saying 'Hallo
to you in your hammock to have one in the garden is Good luck!*
'All is energy ~ match the frequency to the reality of what you want'

<u>Nisargadatta Maharaj</u>
*'Mind is interested in what happens, while awareness ~
is interested in the mind itself. The child is after the toy,
but the mother watches the child, not the toy. Watch your
thoughts and watch yourself watching the thoughts.
The state of freedom from all thoughts will happen
suddenly and by the bliss of it you shall recognise it'*

*

<u>To the Fires of Venus</u>
We All occupy One Infinite Space
*We are all in the Universe together**
"I never stopped loving you"
<Human Artificial Dream Worlds>
*Born into an Invisible Prison of
your designed Sub-Conscious.
A CONTROLLED * NEURAL
*BRAIN*WASHING* SIMULATION APP.
Pulling full AI. Illusions, being less human!
A Super Natural, Petite Red Hot Cruiser!
"You danced the pain away"
Over your Mind's-eye.
Action of Kindness
Telling the Truth!*

*

<u>Life In Harmony</u>
*Intra * Venus ~ Signaling the happy muscle
Chasing * Dreams ~ Coming into a Love Temple.
Sun worshipper on her knees
Just let it run through you
There Is No Separation
Open Heart ~ All Is Love
Transcendence of Enchantment
All in One Infinite Space*

ABOUT SUNNY JETSUN

Inspired by the sixties Sunny started traveling the world in 1970. His spiritual journey on the hippie trail to India took him through San Francisco, Los Angeles, London, Amsterdam, Paris, Vancouver, Sidney, and Kathmandu to Varanasi. His arrival on the sub-continent was the beginning of writing autobiographical verses capturing his travel experiences, encounters with remarkable people and his quest for self-realization. Combining experimentation with drugs, sex, rock & roll, meditation, Love and life in general. Sunny started to open up to a multi-dimensional Universe. He lived the mantra, "Turn on, tune in, drop out" realising Mind's-illusions, inspired by deeper feelings of holistic nature, empathy, energy & Space.

Over four decades Sunny has written and published 27 books of poetry, created over one hundred paintings, traveled the World and considers his masterpiece to be his daughter. He has spent the past fifteen years in Goa, India inspired by the freedom to experience and idealism of human consciousness.

Sunny Jetsun books and art are available on the web at:

Website: www.sunnyjetsun.com
Facebook: www.facebook.com/sunnyjetsun
Amazon: www.amazon.com/author/sunnyjetsun
Smashwords: www.smashwords.com/profile/view/sunnyjetsun

www.ingramcontent.com/pod-product-compliance
Lightning Source LLC
Chambersburg PA
CBHW020505030426
42337CB00011B/233